THE
NICHOLAS NICKLEBY
STORY

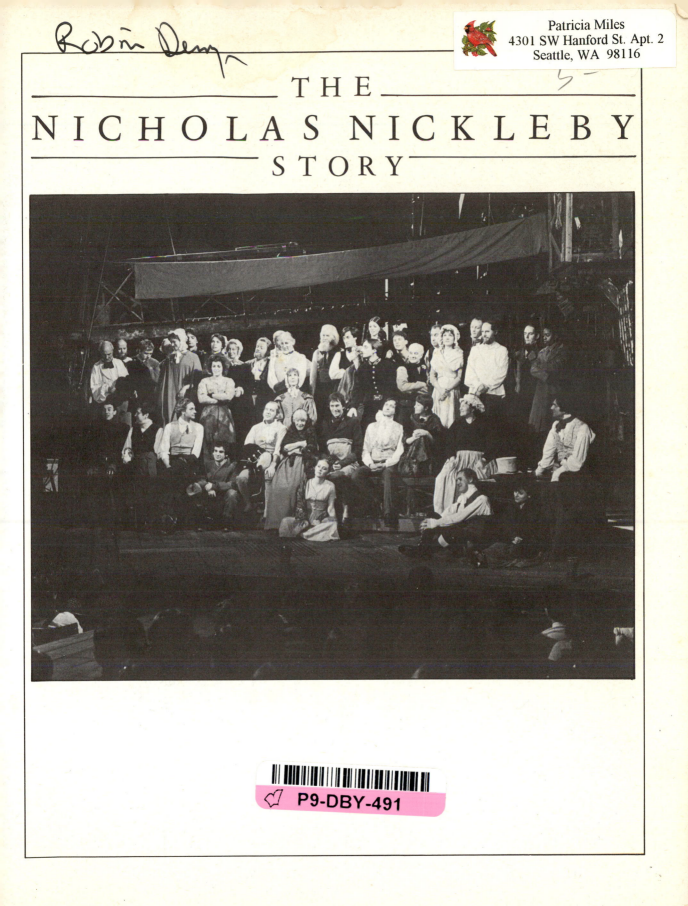

THE NICHOLAS NICKLEBY STORY

LEON RUBIN

THE MAKING OF THE HISTORIC
ROYAL SHAKESPEARE COMPANY PRODUCTION

PENGUIN BOOKS

Penguin Books Ltd, Harmondsworth, Middlesex, England
Penguin Books, 625 Madison Avenue, New York, New York 10022, U.S.A.
Penguin Books Australia Ltd, Ringwood, Victoria, Australia
Penguin Books Canada Ltd, 2801 John Street, Markham, Ontario, Canada L3R 1B4
Penguin Books (N.Z.) Ltd, 182–190 Wairau Road, Auckland 10, New Zealand

First published in Great Britain by William Heinemann Ltd 1981
First published in the United States of America by Penguin Books Ltd 1981

© Leon Rubin 1981
Illustrations © London Weekend Television 1980 and © Chris Davies 1980
All rights reserved

Printed in Great Britain by Morrison & Gibb Ltd., London and Edinburgh
Set in Garamond

Designed by Ginni Moo-Young

The author and publisher would like to thank Granada Publishing Ltd for permission to use an
extract from *The Empty Space* by Peter Brook..

FOR THE NICHOLAS NICKLEBY COMPANY AND MARTINE

AUTHOR'S NOTE

The full list of people I wish to thank would be too long to detail now. It includes many members of the acting company. In particular, Trevor Nunn, Roger Rees, David Edgar and John Caird have all generously helped me to remember facts and details, in addition to sharing with me some of their own feelings about the many months of work on *Nicholas Nickleby*. Andrew Snell, Jamie Muir and Elizabeth Queenan and the staff at London Weekend Television have always been most helpful and kind. Without the advice and support of David Brierley, Peter Harlock, Debbie Horsfield and the rest of the staff at the Royal Shakespeare Company, the book would not have been possible.

I would like to thank London Weekend Television for their photographs by Simon Farrell and Tony Russel. Especially, I am indebted to Chris Davies for allowing me extensive access to all his excellent pictures. And I need to thank my dedicated editor Judith Elliott, my book designer Ginni Moo-Young and my typist Sarah Spare.

This is a very personal view of the work on *Nicholas Nickleby* and I know that many of my colleagues would have written a very different account. Many have helped me write the book, but none are to blame for the opinions I have expressed.

Leon Rubin
London 1981

CONTENTS

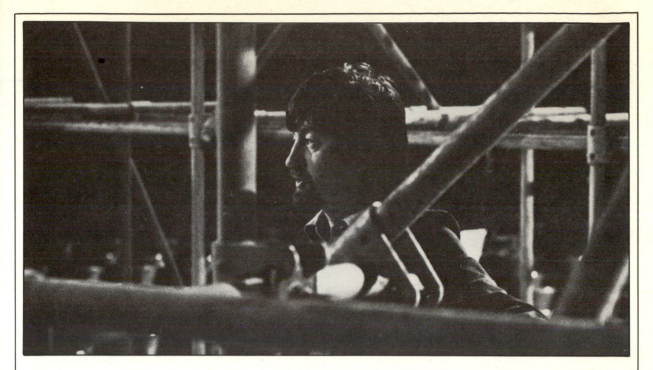

PROLOGUE

The story begins in 1977 when Trevor Nunn, Artistic Director of the Royal Shakespeare Company, set out on a cultural visit to the USSR. At the Gorky Theatre in Leningrad he met his counterpart Tovstonogov, and was surprised to learn that the company were working on an adaptation of *Pickwick Papers*. He was even more surprised to hear that they intended to spend six months preparing it. Tovstonogov explained that it was common to adapt Dickens for the stage in the USSR, where he is one of the most popular novelists. When asked about our own versions of Dickens, Trevor had to admit that the major companies in England had never embarked on such an enterprise, and he remembered a conversation the year before with Peter McEnery, when the actor had expressed his amazement that no full-scale stage adaptation had been attempted.

On a hot summer day at the end of August 1979, when I was the weary assistant director of the Royal Shakespeare Company in Stratford, I had arranged an interview with Trevor Nunn. It is easier to break into the Kremlin than to see Trevor before he wants to see you, but finally, after many weeks of waiting, whilst he directed a play in London, I was going to confront him with my desire to direct my own work, and my refusal to work on anyone else's productions. There is not much left over for oneself after eight months' exhausting work on other directors' plays, however good or bad they might be. My head abounded with images of decapitated bodies from *Cymbeline*, battlefields strewn with corpses from *Julius Caesar*, and strangled necks from *Othello*. After working six and sometimes seven days a week from morning to night, I was very tired and determined never to work again as an assistant director. I had argued, provoked, debated and supported; but in the end I did not feel responsible for the production that emerged. I wanted only my own production.

The mood I was in was fairly typical of the acting company as well. They were all gloomily contemplating the oncoming winter in Stratford. After the opening of our final production of the year, *Julius Caesar*, they would continue playing in the same shows until February, when they would all move with the same productions to Newcastle for six weeks for our annual season there.

As I waited a few minutes before my interview, I gazed out of the window of the Green Room in the theatre at Stratford. An American tourist asked me for my autograph, mistaking me for one of the actors. That was the last straw. I was determined to get what I wanted.

An hour later, I'd been told about the talk with Tovstonogov. I also knew that when Trevor had said, "Well, it's a difficult script," I was not likely to direct my proposed production of Shakespeare and Fletcher's *The Two Noble Kinsmen* in the very near future. Even if a part of the plan that Trevor had outlined to me came to pass, there would be no room for any other new work at all for a long time.

Trevor had invited me to join him and John Caird, his co-director, to form a directorial team for a new project. My first reaction, of cynicism, transformed slowly to excitement when he unveiled his plan to attempt something completely new for the Royal Shakespeare Company. We would try to adapt an entire novel for the stage: an entire work by Dickens, complete with hundreds of characters, multiple plots, narrative and authorial comment; and we would use the whole Stratford company for that end.

The three of us, Trevor and John as co-directors and myself as assistant director, would have to work more closely together than any of us had imagined. I would share the directing with not just one but two directors, one of whom, Trevor Nunn, I knew a little and the other, John Caird, I did not know at all. That was the part of the offer I had most doubts about—not the material itself. However, Trevor promised a collective approach that would not only need three of us as directors, but even then might well prove much bigger than we could at that moment conceive. We would need a collective effort of extraordinary scope from all involved in the project, if we were to stand even a chance of success.

Trevor had wanted to commit the RSC to an epic work for some time. Often, over a period of many years of planning at the RSC, he had thought how few plays really fully exploited all the resources of such a company. Apart from certain Gorky plays or works such as *Bartholomew Fair*, there are not many that stretch and utilise all that was at the RSC's disposal. On holiday he had once read out aloud to Janet Suzman, his wife, the whole of *Little Dorrit* and had been impressed by its dramatic qualities. Again, there was a feeling that Dickens might be the source for that epic project that he had in mind.

Finance also played a key role. By that day in August 1979, the RSC was in grave financial trouble. They had an accumulated deficit of over £200,000, with estimates of a further £200,000 coming by the end of the financial year. With the usual outgoings and projected box office income the total could reach half a million pounds. This would have been an intolerable burden on the board of Governors, who were ultimately liable for that debt. The normal two-year cycle at the RSC begins with a repertory in Stratford, moves to Newcastle for six weeks, and finally arrives in London for a season. The same basic material is played in each venue, although the contracts of the company expire after the season in Newcastle. In order to continue with the Shakespeare work, with as much of the original company as possible, new productions are added at the Aldwych in London, to provide fresh stimulation for the actors. With the deficit that the RSC were now facing it was not possible to sustain the London season. The only solution seemed to be to close the Aldwych in September. But if that happened there was a good chance that the Arts Council grant would also be cut accordingly, and the RSC would be back where they started, still in debt with half the company operation severed off.

The Arts Council implied that the increase in grant for the next financial year would be only 7 per cent. With inflation at 15 per cent, and moving upward, the outlook was bleak. The only way through from the Newcastle season even to September was for the RSC to trim right back to the minimum of new work. The Shakespeare productions would be already built and ready for the Aldwych and therefore relatively inexpensive to mount, but the usual cost of all the new productions would be saved.

Trevor's philosophy was that the best form of defence is

attack, and he believed that what he needed to find was a single piece of work that would provide a challenging acting opportunity for the entire company. Only in that way could the Shakespeare season survive for a season in London, at least until September. It was at this point that the different Dickens connections seemed to meet in his mind. He decided on an adaptation of a Dickens novel, that would harness in one work all the RSC's vast resources and demonstrate what that company could really achieve.

Trevor consulted two people before that meeting with me. First he sounded out the designer John Napier. Although heavily involved in another enormous project, John Barton's three-part cycle of Greek drama, *The Greeks*, John agreed to take part. Then he talked to John Caird, with whom he had worked closely before on other productions, and asked him to co-direct.

The problem now was to convince everyone in the acting company to take the risk and commit themselves to such a work. With, as yet, no script and consequently no parts to offer there was little for them to base their decision on. There could also be no guarantees of work, even with *Nicholas Nickleby*, beyond September. Probably, no other new work could be offered in addition to this.

In September, Trevor called a company meeting to explain the financial situation and propose the project, stressing its special experimental nature. He was offering everyone in that company a re-engagement until next September. Everyone who wanted to could be in it. However, the offer would, by necessity, be two-way. No casting or offers could yet be made, but anyone who walked through the door on the first day of rehearsal was committed.

Reactions were very mixed. Many of the company seemed exhilarated about the possibilities inherent in the proposal, many others looked wary and cynical. A large number of the company would not normally accept any acting engagement without a specific part to read through first. After playing Malvolio, Brutus, Olivia or Iago it is something of a surprise to have to risk playing very little in a new work, with no security of employment a few months later. But those were the terms.

The next few days were spent in frantic novel-reading, at least by those who were able to find a copy of *Nicholas Nickleby* in the Stratford library or bookshops! Through a series of conversations that I had with the company I knew that many of them were still very unhappy with the offer. The terms seemed too harsh. Some actors phoned Trevor in London to express their fears. He agreed to have another meeting a few days later, to which anyone who had further questions to ask could come. Meanwhile, he talked to many of the actors' agents, some of whom were extremely suspicious of the proposal, and explained the reasoning behind it.

About twenty people turned up at the second meeting. Now the offer was modified, for the benefit of those who still had anxieties. There must still be a commitment from those who began work on *Nicholas Nickleby*, but after five weeks of trial, experimental work they could, if they desired, leave. Similarly, the directors would also have the right to cancel the project at that point. Now the company would go away and think carefully for another three days, and consult their agents. We hoped that our assurances had succeeded, for that was the final offer.

After those final three days we would wait in the rehearsal room, with an open door, and see who turned up. I feared there might be only a few. Casual conversations suggested that many people had yet to make up their minds. I would just have to wait and see.

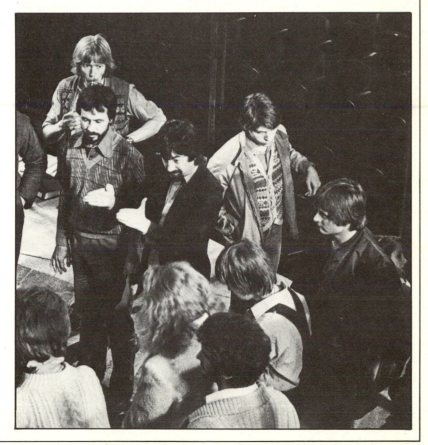

THE CIRCLE FORMS

The Nicholas Nickleby Company

Nicholas Nickleby was the novel Trevor read right at the beginning of his search for an appropriate Dickens work to adapt. He was quickly convinced that it would work, but first he wanted to compare it with other Dickens novels. He also asked John Caird to read various novels that might be possible choices. *David Copperfield, Oliver Twist* and *Dombey and Son* were soon ruled out.

One of the most interesting novels seemed to be *Our Mutual Friend*, but the dominating presence of the River Thames, which is geographically and symbolically at the centre of so many of the events in the novel, presented too many theatrical problems.

Bleak House was another strong contender, and since Trevor had not read it, it was agreed that John, who has a remarkable memory, should recount the story to him. He soon discovered what a difficult task it was. As he worked his way through the complexities of multiple plots and themes, he found that before he could adequately retell it he had to come to terms with the essential meaning behind the novel. It was not possible just to give a simple plot skeleton. This experience led to John suggesting the first experimental exercise for the company in which they would collectively try to retell the story of *Nicholas Nickleby* to each other.

Hard Times was also a possibility. It is carefully structured and highly focused, unlike some of Dickens's longer and somewhat unwieldy works. It contains a fine collection of characters and has a clearly defined social intention behind the story. However, a brilliant television version directed by John Irvine made John and Trevor feel that it had already been excellently adapted and therefore that they should focus on a different novel.

Knowing the particular Stratford company that he had, Trevor felt sure that *Nicholas Nickleby* was the best vehicle for their particular range of talents. In addition he was attracted to the picaresque form in which it is written. The life and adventures of Nicholas Nickleby take the reader on a long and eventful journey through many different environments: the cold dark corridors of Dotheboys Hall; the lavish showrooms of Madame Mantalini's millinery establishments; the extravagant and eccentric theatre company of Mr Crummles; the business chambers of Ralph Nickleby; the debtor's house of the King's Bench Prison; the aristocratic club of Sir Mulberry Hawk; the two rooms of the Kenwigs family and the larger rooms of the Wittiterlies. The bewildering experiences that Nicholas endures allow him contact with all strata of nineteenth-century English society. This process of journey and adventure seemed a good basis for adaptation for the stage. The central character would act as a focus for the vast series of events and characters in the novel, and would be a unifying factor.

In *Nicholas Nickleby*, Dickens explores a full cross-section of the social classes of nineteenth-century England with all their strengths, weaknesses and affectations. In particular, he centres on the theme of money: money as a corrupting force and money as a means of doing good. He continually compares and contrasts different attitudes towards money within and between each social group, weaving this theme through his analysis of class structures and attitudes.

There is also a strong emotional centre to the novel in the character of Smike. Through Smike and his journey and adventures with Nicholas, Dickens explores his favourite topic: the nature of humanity in the world. In spite of the sufferings Smike undergoes and the degradations he has to endure, humanity is still to be found in the novel alive and kicking, although sometimes arriving late.

Nicholas Nickleby is also a work of exceptional vitality, combining a detailed social critique with an array of dazzling acting vehicles, and providing a wonderful source of dramatic possibility. Unlike a more consistently earnest work such as *Dombey and Son*, it swings rapidly back and forth between tragedy and comedy and all the shades of mood between. Dickens constantly juxtaposes scenes of laughter and sadness and retains a humorous sense of proportion through even the most serious scenes.

In addition, there is the Crummles Theatre subplot in the novel which would provide a natural rich source of acting opportunities for the company. Those scenes would also necessitate a serious analysis of attitudes towards acting style in the nineteenth century and the present day. The questions provoked by actors pretending to be Dickens's actors acting would be fascinating and of central importance to the work as a whole. It is interesting that Dickens loved theatre and dedicated *Nicholas Nickleby* to his friend the great Victorian actor W. C. Macready.

Having decided on the novel, the next problem was to find a writer. However collective the rehearsals might turn out to be, we would need an extraordinary writer to create a script from over nine hundred pages of text. He or she would have to be a playwright in their own right as well as an experienced and highly literate adaptor. David Edgar was the first name that came to mind, although none of us had worked with him before. He had completed various successful adaptations in the recent past; the most recent two were *Mary Barnes* and *The Jail Diary of Albie Sachs* for the RSC. David seemed to be the best qualified and even looked the part—a large, round, bespectacled man with the face of an over-intelligent schoolboy—another perfect addition to our Dickensian collection. Although at that moment he was in the USA up to his neck in another project, he agreed to join us a few days into rehearsal.

Trevor knew a little about David through some earlier correspondence. A few months earlier he had talked to Cecil Clark from ATV about a film he wanted to direct, using the Stratford company, some time in the autumn. He had decided on an adaptation of *Felix Holt* by George Eliot, and had asked David, already then in the USA, if he would like to adapt it. David accepted the offer and wrote a long letter about the whole question of adaptation, about the immense responsibility that he felt to the work of a dead writer, and how he suffered over having to make the changes that were necessary for adaptation. Trevor was impressed by David's attitude and replied at length. Now, some months later, he felt somewhat self-conscious at proposing a change of text and a shift from film to the stage, but nevertheless felt sure that David was the right man.

This was the team—"the Gang of Four" as we were later

dubbed, as we were seen arguing together in late-night restaurants throughout the year to come. The other person to join us soon after was Stephen Oliver, the composer. Trevor had worked with him on previous productions for the RSC, *Romeo and Juliet* and *As You Like It*. He writes about an opera a week in his spare time, when not writing incidental theatre music. His encyclopaedic musical knowledge and his ability to write very fast were to prove invaluable, as we were later to find out only too well.

As we sit in the Conference Hall on the first day of rehearsal I am curious to know how many will come to join us. It is ten-thirty in the morning. The first faces start to appear, looking in to see who else is here. Within twenty minutes the room is filled with actors and actresses. Everywhere we look there seems to be another member of the Stratford company. Out of a total company of sixty, four of whom we know are not available, forty-six actors and actresses have walked into the room.

We were all still tired; but now there was something that might offer an alternative to our normal rhythm of work. Maybe that is why so many were there. There is so much wrong with the usual pattern of work in most theatres in this country. A few weeks rushed rehearsal, and a few hectic days of technical preparation before the public arrives. The RSC is fortunate in comparison to most. An RSC production has about six weeks rehearsal—a luxurious amount of time compared with many repertory theatres—but in those six weeks it is so rarely possible to achieve greatness. Even with all the care and love and attention that goes into rehearsal day after day, the texts of the great works defy such a process; they are too vast to come to terms with in such a short time. With actors and actresses performing four or five other works at the same time, energy is spread very thin in many directions. Directors and actors frequently have to come to Shakespearean work, for example, with fixed ideas; it is not easy in a few weeks to escape from old associations and images. The conditions of rehearsal are geared too much to production, not enough towards exploration and understanding of the material itself. Through financial pressures, many theatres have to turn out one production after another every few weeks, and become just another cog in the big wheel of the machine of the entertainment industry. It continually amazes me how much excellent work is achieved, in spite of underfinancing and enforced rushed rehearsals, in our repertory theatres and fringe companies. At the other extreme, also trapped by the financial system, there is much of the commercial West End theatre with its collection of long-running, moribund productions, kept on month after month and year after year to eventual death. The great Royal Shakespeare Company Shakespearean productions like Peter Brook's *Dream*, Terry Hands' *Henry V*, Trevor Nunn's *Macbeth* and *The Wars of the Roses*, to name but a very few, are some of the exceptions. They live dynamically through the genius of the actors and directors involved, in spite of the conditions of rehearsal. I re-read Peter Brook's *The Empty Space* before the first rehearsal day.

> The problem of the Deadly Theatre is like the problem of the deadly bore. Every deadly bore has head, heart, arms, legs; usually he has a family and friends; he even has his admirers. Yet we sigh when we come across him—and in this sigh we are regretting that somehow he is at the bottom instead of the top of his possibilities. When we say deadly, we never mean dead: we mean something depressingly active, but for this very reason capable of change. The first step towards this change is facing the simple unattractive fact that most of what is called theatre anywhere in the world is a travesty of a word once full of sense. War or peace, the colossal bandwagon of culture trundles on, carrying each artist's traces to the evermounting garbage heap. Theatres, actors, critics and public are interlocked in a machine that creaks, but never stops. There is always a new season in hand and we are too busy to ask the only vital question which measures the whole structure. Why theatre at all? What for? Is it an anachronism, a superannuated oddity, surviving like an old monument or a quaint custom? Why do we applaud, and what? Has the stage a real place in our lives? What function can it have? What could it serve? What could it explore? What are its special properties?
>
> In Mexico, before the wheel was invented, gangs of slaves had to carry giant stones through the jungle and up the mountains, while their children pulled their toys on tiny rollers. The slaves made the toys, but for centuries failed to make the connection. When good actors play in bad comedies or second-rate musicals, when audiences applaud indifferent classics because they enjoy the costumes or just the way the sets change, or just the prettiness of the leading actress, there is nothing wrong. But none the less, have they noticed what is underneath the toy they are dragging on a string? It's a wheel.

I, and I believe many others, were hoping then from that first day of rehearsal for a new, fresh approach to work and a new set of rehearsal conditions. Many significant changes had already been made. The first was that we had chosen a new work, something that had never before been done in a complete form on the stage. The second change was the absence of a known script; we had to write the adaptation as we went along. And the third was a large collection of senior and younger actors mixed together, working in a project without knowing specifically what they would play. Already most of our normal rules had been broken. Many others, I hoped, would also soon disappear.

We met to rehearse in the Conference Hall, the main rehearsal space at Stratford. It is a large, oblong room with a semi-circular alcove at one end in which there are two staircases that wind down from a raised platform to meet each other near the centre. In the ceiling are a series of skylights that allow daylight in—an important factor in creating the wonderful working atmosphere that we always feel when rehearsing there. That rehearsal room is all that is left of the first Shakespeare Memorial Theatre that burnt down in 1926. It was the first of very many different spaces in Stratford, Newcastle and London in which we would all rehearse.

In the centre of the Conference Hall we start to form a large circle of chairs. A mad search for extra seats takes place, and we drag in various battered settees and armchairs from earlier productions, previously considered retired. It had been a long time back in the RSC's work that such a large group of actors and directors had worked together in that room. The large discussion circle is a pattern that will stay with us for a long time.

As the forty-nine of us plus the stage management team of three sit and look at each other in the circle, the five-week trial period starts. The company waits, curiously, to see how it will begin.

Trevor and John had prepared a three-part structure for the first period of rehearsals. The plan was to focus on three areas of exploration: 1) Background; 2) Narrative; 3) Character. The background would be explored by a method often employed by Trevor and some other directors at the beginning of a rehearsal period. The company would be asked to research topics concerning the social background of the period in which the novel was written, and the important facts concerning Dickens himself. Discussions following these reports would concentrate on other connecting areas of nineteenth-century life and attitudes.

The narrative aspects of the adapting process would centre on finding ways of storytelling. The first exercise would be derived from John's experience of trying to retell *Bleak House* to Trevor.

The character work would explore, through various exercises, individual characters in the novel, and the company's relationship to them.

We began with the narrative plan. Every actor was allocated a chapter or two of the novel to read, with the specific intention of retelling the contents of it later to the rest of the group. This would all take place in one session in a few days. In the meantime the background and character work were also to begin.

The company were asked to embark on a massive research exercise. We wanted to find out everything we could about Dickens and his world, immersing ourselves totally in the period and erasing false images from our minds before forming our own attitude towards the people and events in the novel. John Caird produced a carefully organised list of subjects: Charles Dickens's life—Victorian theatre—London in the 1830s—music — government — sport — food — health — medicine — economics—the underworld—education—the opera—general politics — royalty — literature — class structure — work — wages —newspaper headlines—sexual habits and attitudes, and so on.

As the next five weeks passed by, an extraordinarily detailed picture of Victorian life in the 1830s emerged. We would return to our circle every few days to hear more of the fruits of the research. The keener researchers produced pages and pages of work. We heard about what people ate and the poisons that were used to colour their food, the politics that they debated and the music that they loved. Rose Hill, the oldest female member of the company, trained in her youth as an opera singer and she sang to us a popular romantic song of the day. Roderick Horn played us some Victorian opera.

Roger Rees became obsessed with the fact that the Victorians used long tablecloths to cover up the tables completely, so that unsuspecting persons would not be caused sexual embarrassment looking at table legs.

Willoughby Goddard, a keen amateur historian, happily immersed himself in days of research and produced for us a detailed account of relations between government and royalty.

Bob Peck spent two days relating to us a vast and rich account of pastimes and sports of the period. He led us from the genteel parlour games to aristocratic casinos and smoke-filled dog-fighting dens and the racetrack. Sports and pastimes spilled over into a grim analysis of the whole underworld life of the time.

Cathryn Harrison, a bright twenty-one-year-old actress who had been in film and television before the RSC, offered eagerly to research health and medicine. Cathryn's feelings were typical of many of the younger members of the company. She had been a popular actress playing leading roles on film, who suddenly found herself at the beginning again, with the Royal Shakespeare Company. Giving up a film career to move on to the stage is a painful process. Having acted since she was a young child, she had always done well. She knew that without stage experience she would be in small roles at the RSC, but it was even worse than she expected. Shakespeare is particularly unkind territory for young actresses. There's not much in the middle ground between ladies-in-waiting and whores on one side, or Juliet and Miranda on the other. Cathryn had done her fair share of the former roles when "Nicholas" was first conceived. So, keen to discover a new type of work, with enthusiasm and good humour she jumped, so to speak, headlong into the murky Victorian world of open sewers in the streets, venereal disease, infant mortality and malnutrition-twisted limbs. When Nicholas is admired by Fanny Squeers for his straight legs, it is not a joke. He would have been about the only one in Dotheboys Hall who was healthy enough to stand straight. Cathryn horrified us all with her details of the ignorance and neglect that caused premature death and illness in so many people of that time. The gruesome descriptions of everyday life began to explain to us some of our images of Victorian England that we so easily misunderstood. The crippled and disfigured characters in Dickens's novels are not grotesque caricatures, but helpless, sad human beings drawn from real life.

We were given a second lesson and proof of Dickens's social realism when we heard about the education system of the 1830s, and the description of the "Yorkshire schools", the notorious schools on which Dotheboys Hall was modelled. Dickens the journalist had visited such a school to research his novel; as we heard from the press reports of the period, we learned that Dotheboys Hall was not exceptional in its brutality or fictional in its detail, but typical. Even Mr Squeers the schoolmaster was depicted after the headmaster of a school near Greta Bridge in Yorkshire. Many months later two of the company, Roger Rees and David Threlfall, visited the site of the school at Greta Bridge in Yorkshire and interviewed on tape a local resident who pointed out where old Squeers used to live as if he no longer knew fiction from history. After the report about education we debated for many hours about Dickens the social reformer. Was he a radical, or did he merely jump on the bandwagon from reports that had already appeared in many papers before the publication of *Nicholas Nickleby*?

Two sessions in particular were important to us in our later work. The first was a lesson in basic economics and the value of money. Through a practical enacted demonstration we were taught how the bill of exchange was the cornerstone of financial transactions in that period. Like a mongrel version of a cheque and an IOU, this form of money was the key to the fortunes and fates of many businessmen. Ralph Nickleby founded his wealth upon it, and the Mantalini family are destroyed by it. But, even more important, we learned the true value and importance of money. A typical poor family with five children, with parents working long hours every week, had to live on less than a pound a week with no social support. Unemployment meant starvation, and unemployment was high, due to the cruelties and follies of the attitudes of the period—not so different from the monetarist theories of our own time. From that moment on, all mention of money or financial transactions was of special interest to us. Much later in our work, during an argument, David Edgar was challenged by Trevor to say what he thought *Nicholas Nickleby* was really about. He replied, "Money".

The other important session was provided by Edward Petherbridge and Emily Richard. Edward, gentle and serious, with his mime-trained body that he moves so gracefully, his love of theatre history, and his belief in the power of reasonable behaviour and the importance of justice, would prove invaluable to *Nicholas Nickleby* later, when the pressure was on. Together with Emily, a petite, dark, wide-eyed actress with a deep and penetrating voice, he offered us a magic lantern performance on Victorian theatre, unlocking for us with slides and tapes the world of Victorian theatre. We all began to feel a warmth and excitement towards these actors and their theatre as Edward and Emily focused on a cartoon illustration of the life and fortunes of a typical actor of the period. As the smiling company watched the history of hard times and unemployment of the actor Proteus, in a book by Pearce Egan written in 1825, they knew that the world of Crummles's theatre was not so far from their own.

There were those amongst the actors who felt that what they thought was going to be a rehearsal had turned into a seminar. "Our own university," said Willoughby Goddard with pride. "Too much talking, I'm going crazy," said David Lloyd Meredith. However, research and discussions were just a small part of our Dickensian immersion process, and Trevor encouraged the process further.

Between the hearings of research papers, another series of discussions took place. What do we think of when we think of Dickens? What are our impressions and visual images, and where do they come from? We wanted to discover the roots of the Dickensian consciousness. Dickens, like Shakespeare, is so much a part of our cultural heritage that it is difficult to remember a time in our lives when we were unaware of his existence. Although we do not always remember the novels by name, we recall them by association with the characters or the words they speak. Dickens has become an institution more than a novelist. We often use the word "Dickensian" to describe an essentially secondhand view of Dickens based on sentiment and affection, whereas, in his own lifetime, Dickens was seen as a radical writer of extreme moral views.

Some of the senior members of the company quickly formulated detailed Dickensian memories. Many of them, such as Norman Tyrrell, distinctly remember Dickens being read to them in their family at home when they were children.

Hubert Rees, one of the strong Welsh contingent in the company, had recollections of fear. He remembered fragments of frightening scenes and frightening characters, although he was not sure exactly which works they came from. He had an early visual memory of an old Hollywood film of *The Old Curiosity Shop* from which he could still remember specific moments. And he had vaguer recollections of Dickens being read to him.

Willoughby Goddard, now aged fifty-three, remembered *Oliver Twist* being thrust into his hands when he was very ill at the age of eight. From that moment on, he had an immense love for Dickens. Fagin was his hero for many years after and he loved Fagin for being so kind to Oliver when he was needed. He remembers reading *Pickwick Papers* every Christmas for years.

Roger Rees had extraordinarily detailed Mayhewesque memories of Dickens in his childhood. He was brought up near Clapham Junction and recalled that Dickens gave him his first awareness of what the sounds meant of the trains rolling past. He used to sit and play on coal lorries, and it was after reading Dickens that he understood that they belonged to the real world, and real people worked on them. Dickens, he is quite sure, gave him the beginning of his social awareness. He also remembered that at twelve he was given, as a divinity prize, *Oliver Twist, Pickwick Papers* and *Nicholas Nickleby*, and read them all with great relish.

All I could remember was vague, dull, brown and white tinted photographs of strange faces with long noses and exaggerated eyes. I didn't know whether they were Phiz drawings or from any other source but I did know that it was the visual memory that had been triggered in me first.

Most of the younger members of the company recalled black and white images from old film versions and television adaptations of Dickens.

As we moved around the circle, we heard again and again memories of specific characters, specific incidents, but few if any of us could recall more than fragments. As we went through our later memories and images of Dickens, we still found that it was character that emerged clear and strong whereas plot, theme and moral purpose had faded far away. The eccentric and extraordinary characters had marked our memories permanently but something essential had vanished. Dickens the social commentator, Dickens the angry man, Dickens the journalist, Dickens the moralist was absent from our collective memory. Nearly all our visual images centred on black and white or brown and white fragments; murky, dark interiors, dusty offices and narrow winding streets. What was missing was the teeming, bright, dynamic world of Dickens's Victorian England, bursting forth with energy and industry and belief in itself. The vigorously active society uncovered by our research had been forgotten. But, much more important than that, the essential motivation behind the novels had also been forgotten. The soul of the work had been obscured by the overpowering presence of Mrs Gamp, Fagin and Little Nell. The Phiz illustrations perpetuate the same distortions, and even recent cinematic images go back to that same source. We knew that one of our first tasks would be to try and rediscover the lost Dickens and collectively remember why the novels were written in the first place. We would have to explore the parts of the novel normally ignored in dramatisations.

Most adaptations for the stage, television or film present the characters but because of length and dramatic focus, simplify the plots. Even more important, they ignore the words between the incidents; the narrative and descriptive sections and the intrusive moments of authorial comment. Yet these passages are the quintessential Dickens at work. Therefore, from the sharing of memories and impressions we begin to feel that it was the gaps, the void between character and incident, that we must explore in our search for a dramatisation of an entire novel.

In the evenings after rehearsal Trevor, John and I began the habit of looking back at each day's work and planning the next. From these early discussions onwards, we felt that the greatest danger in all of our work was, ironically, the love of the Phiz characters that all the company felt. We believed that the caricature figures of Phiz were the most important images to avoid. Actors love eccentric characters: they are always a joy to play. We felt that it was the real and complex people behind the characters that we had to get close to. If we could do this, the dangers of melodrama and sentimental indulgence could be avoided. Victorian melodrama, so strong in the novel of *Nicholas Nickleby*, is perilous territory for a modern audience. All credibility can vanish in a few moments of inappropriate laughter: we had to deal somehow with the death of Smike.

We had also begun to explore the physical side of the work with the company. The discussions and research papers were completed alongside the beginning of other forms of exercises. But how do you begin rehearsal with nearly fifty actors and no script?

David Edgar had joined us and widened our circle, but he had been asked by Trevor not to begin any writing for some time. The plan was to find improvisatory techniques that might begin to provide a method of approach for some of the most difficult areas of the novel, in particular the narrative sections that would in most adaptations be considered essentially non-dramatic, and therefore omitted.

David Edgar, John Caird and Leon Rubin

27

Trevor outlined to the company his own understanding of the way in which forms of improvisation might be used. To this end he summarised what he considers to be two basic forms of improvisation: Stanislavskian and Brechtian. In the former, a situation is created and then explored by actors in character. Then, the characters themselves are asked to work out a conclusion and resolution. Stanislavskian exercises require an actor to immerse himself in a character and allow the character to take on a life of his own. Brechtian improvisation, however, provides a situation and uses characters only as a means of reaching a pre-defined end, of solving a problem or coming to terms with certain questions. Trevor declared that for our work the Brechtian process of improvisation would be the appropriate choice.

Edward Petherbridge expressed his general dislike of improvisations, largely caused by unfortunate past experiences. One or two other members of the company had similar misgivings. To my surprise, one of the more unconventional actors, David Threlfall, explained his aversion to being asked to improvise a character he did not yet really know much about. Trevor reiterated that nothing of that sort would be required, and fears were thus allayed, although I felt that our options had been narrowed by this distinction and choice.

THE BALL OF STRING

The company mime "wealth and poverty . . . repletion and starvation"

Whilst Trevor, John, David and I were discussing our next strategy, we had the results of the storytelling exercise. Moving round the circle, from one actor to another, the story was created chapter by chapter.

Many of us felt that the result was generally tedious. The story itself was dull. The storytellers, reading their hastily précis'd plot, became confused about details, especially in the latter half of the novel. It was not just that half of them were retelling a fragment from a whole that they had not yet finished reading, but that they had no point of view. The art of storytelling is centred on the storyteller's involvement with character and plot. He cannot, in James Joyce's words, sit back godlike and pare his fingernails. He must have an attitude towards the contents of his story. Only then can the magic of the story work whilst the storyteller draws his audience into a web until, helpless and trapped, they are compelled to listen.

Some of the company did manage to contact their audience to a degree. In particular, two of the older actors, Griff Jones and Willoughby Goddard, were able to tell their chapters directly, without constant reference to notes. One or two of the other actors and actresses told their chapters with charm and humour, but on the whole the problems overshadowed the successes.

Trevor felt fascinated and instructed by the process. He thought that it had been an excellent introduction for us all to the vastness of the work. Its full scope was now clearly revealed. Also, he felt that it had indicated the particular plot difficulties inherent in the second half of the novel. The most well-known sections of the novel, Dotheboys Hall and the Crummles Theatre Company sequence, were over before even the halfway point in the novel was reached.

The session lasted an hour and three-quarters whilst the sixty-five chapters were recounted, but it seemed much longer.

The discussions suggested that the central problem was connected to that lack of point of view. There had not been a sufficient grasp of the moral purpose behind the story. The only solution was to do it all again, with a modified brief. Each actor was to retell the story, this time as though he himself was the storyteller, with a viewpoint of his own. More detail and, possibly, dialogue would be used to show the attitude of the characters toward each other and the events. Still, however, the exercise was to be kept to a minimum length.

A few days later we returned to our storytelling circle. This time it took nearly seven hours. We began to feel what the story was really about; we were moved and angered and delighted and saddened as we listened to Nicholas's adventures on his journey through England. Many of the actors had prepared and learnt their stories this time and they met other people's eyes as they told their story. Each chapter was a story in itself and yet part of an inseparable whole.

Even after this second telling of the story, there were many areas of specific plot detail that were blurred. We spent another day checking back in the novel, clarifying loose ends early in the story itself and sometimes inventing our own story to fill the gaps. We found that even Dickens had left some ends untied. In particular the financial plot, centred around Ralph Nickleby, was unclear. What happened to the money that Ralph Nickleby invested in the beginning in the United Metropolitan Improved Hot Muffin and Crumpet Baking and Punctual Delivery Company? Why does the death of Lord Verisopht destroy Sir Mulberry Hawk? What was the financial collapse mysteriously mentioned before Ralph's death? David was sure that the answers to these questions would be the line that brought together plot and thematic intent. Whatever else happened in the novel, the financial plot always ran side by side with it.

Between the two exercises of storytelling we all went to see a screening of an old film adaptation of *Oliver Twist*, with Sir Alec Guinness as Fagin and Anthony Newley as the Artful Dodger.

We had it screened in the enormous cinema in Stratford. The

company was alone in the auditorium and we all felt as though we were reliving our youthful visits to the Saturday morning flicks. Our excitement and childlike pleasure was immediately enhanced by the film itself. The film amused and involved the company and made them laugh. It surprised me how much we were gripped by the final rooftop chase with Bill Sykes dragging the hapless Oliver with him.

At the discussion afterwards the company expressed their delight, but, as we analysed more closely what we had seen, Trevor homed in on specific problems. Why threaten Oliver in the first place? Who is the stranger who came looking for him at the workhouse? What was his connection with Mr Bumble? No one in the circle was able to answer these questions. We had to admit that the central plot presented in the film did not make sense. The vital questions asked by Dickens concerning illegitimacy had been deliberately avoided in the film, and the moral purpose and fervour behind the novel had been covered up or lost. Perhaps because of difficulties with length, or as a direct intention to censor, the film-makers had tried to avoid the theme of illegitimacy and consequently blurred the telling of the story. Where the film had succeeded, it had been on the level of character and incident. In many ways that version of *Oliver Twist* could be identified with most of the usual preconceptions that go with our use of the word "Dickensian". Trevor focused the discussion towards this crucial area of analysis as a lead-up to the second storytelling exercise. It was a further evidence of how important it was that the lost areas of Dickens be rediscovered before the work of adapting the entire *Nicholas Nickleby* could begin.

Some days later we screened a second early Dickens film adaptation, *David Copperfield* with W. C. Fields as Micawber. This version was of little help to us by that point. The acting styles of larger-than-life caricature performances seemed to represent all the worst aspects of Dickensian *schtick* that we were all determined to avoid. The plot was grossly simplified and everything was geared to sentiment. It was a good further reminder to us of more so-called "Dickensian" qualities that we had to remove from our minds.

Now, we needed to channel some of these early discoveries about storytelling into a practical exercise. There were strongly mixed feelings among the actors, between enthusiasm for a new shared thinking and working process, and a sense of uncertainty about where it would all lead. One or two began to feel that the process was too slow and, not for the last time in the months that followed, did they mistrust the long and weary process that we had all begun.

One of the first things that Trevor had insisted on was that an entire novel should be adapted. Unlike these earlier Dickens adaptations we wanted to include the "undramatic" passages—the narrative episodes, the moral digressions. All the discussion and work so far suggested that these were the areas that showed the real Dickens at work—the forgotten Dickens.

Now, Trevor and John chose a passage from the novel that was both central to the understanding of Dickens's narrative intention and potentially the most difficult to realise in any dramatic form. We circulated the passage, divided the company into four groups and let them go away into separate rooms and spend a day preparing their own theatrical version of the piece on their own. This would be the first example of what Trevor had defined as a Brechtian improvisation. Our intention was to discover ways in which passages like this, crammed full of complex incident, could be staged without losing the strong moral voice behind the action. We needed to encourage the inventive abilities of the company, and the description of the arrival of the coach, with its flood of images and incidents, would be a perfect testing ground.

Each group was to appoint a chairperson, but no director would be present. We only dropped in on occasional visits to answer particular questions, and I had the feeling that the actors were happier on their own.

This was the passage chosen:

"London at last!" cried Nicholas, throwing back his great-coat and rousing Smike from a long nap. "It seemed to me as though we should never reach it."

"And yet you came along at a tidy pace too," observed the coachman, looking over his shoulder at Nicholas with no very pleasant expression of countenance.

"Ay, I know that," was the reply; "but I have been very anxious to be at my journey's end, and that makes the way seem long."

"Well," remarked the coachman, "if the way seemed long with such cattle as you've sat behind, you *must* have been most uncommon anxious"; and so saying, he let out his whiplash and touched up a little boy on the calves of his legs by way of emphasis.

They rattled on through the noisy, bustling, crowded streets of London, now displaying long double rows of brightly-burning lamps, dotted here and there with the chemists' glaring lights, and illuminated besides with the brilliant flood that streamed from the windows of the shops, where sparkling jewellery, silks and velvets of the richest colours, the most inviting delicacies, and most sumptuous articles of luxurious ornament, succeeded each other in rich

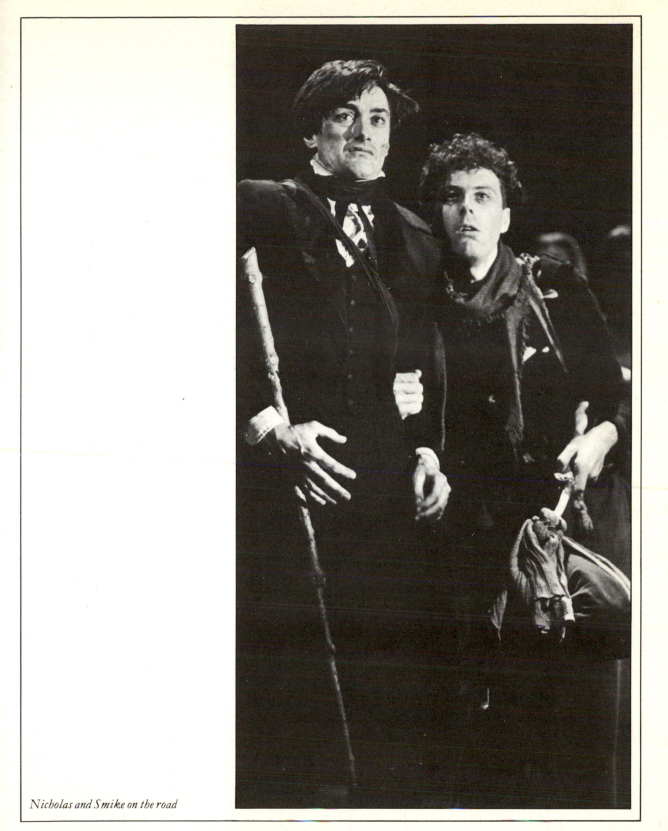

Nicholas and Smike on the road

and glittering profusion. Streams of people apparently without end poured on and on, jostling each other in the crowd and hurrying forward, scarcely seeming to notice the riches that surrounded them on every side; while vehicles of all shapes and makes, mingled up together in one moving mass like running water, lent their ceaseless roar to swell the noise and tumult.

As they dashed by the quickly-changing and ever-varying objects, it was curious to observe in what a strange procession they passed before the eye. Emporiums of splendid dresses, the materials brought from every quarter of the world; tempting stores of everything to stimulate and pamper the sated appetite and give new relish to the oft-repeated feast; vessels of burnished gold and silver, wrought into every exquisite form of vase, and dish, and goblet; guns, swords, pistols, and patent engines of destruction; screws and irons for the crooked, clothes for the newly-born, drugs for the sick, coffins for the dead, and churchyards for the buried—all these jumbled each with the other and flocking side by side, seemed to flit by in motley dance like the fantastic groups of the old Dutch painter, and with the same stern moral for the unheeding restless crowd.

Nor were there wanting objects in the crowd itself to give new point and purpose to the shifting scene. The rags of the squalid ballad-singer fluttered in the rich light that showed the goldsmith's treasures, pale and pinched-up faces hovered about the windows where was tempting food, hungry eyes wandered over the profusion guarded by one thin sheet of brittle glass—an iron wall to them; half-naked shivering figures stopped to gaze at Chinese shawls and golden stuffs of India. There was a christening party at the largest coffin-maker's, and a funeral hatchment had stopped some great improvements in the bravest mansion. Life and death went hand in hand; wealth and poverty stood side by side; repletion and starvation laid them down together.

But it was London; . . .

The directors were due to see all the versions of the text the next day, but as became the pattern for most of our work on *Nicholas Nickleby*, we postponed for another half a day to allow more time.

We sit and wait for the results of the four groups' collective imaginations. The first group sit us, the audience, in the middle of the room and, parts of the text divided amongst them, they run and cartwheel and jump around us, acting out a myriad of visual images in the passage. A grotesque funeral procession is followed by musical acrobatic extravagance and laughter. The actors, egged on by Ben Kingsley, rattle keys to sound like the clanking wheels of a stagecoach as they flow ceaselessly around us. It is an exciting experience to be surrounded by the thronging noise and clamour of a company of people, which launches us right into the middle of Victorian London.

Months later our final design reflected this need for direct contact between actor and audience and the simple ingenuity of improvised sound effects would come back again and again.

The second group, based on mime, seems to be led by Edward Petherbridge. It shows a series of extraordinary images, of crowds of people jostling and bustling their way along. As they reach an agreed point in their movement the mass of bodies fan out into three lines of people facing us, the audience, one line behind the other. In the exaggerated gestures of elegant ladies and gentlemen they genteelly sip their imaginary coffee and eat their food. Suddenly, they turn a slow three hundred and sixty degrees and when they face us again, they are transformed into the poor of London, desperately pressing starved faces and clutching hands at the glass window through which we had just seen the rich people eating their food. The effect is stunning. In one orchestrated moment they have hit on the centre of the passage, the juxtaposition of wealth and poverty, repletion and starvation side by side.

We never forgot that image and it appeared, in a modified form, in the final production many months later.

In the third version, the whole text is divided between actors and actresses, some of them passing copies of the novel back and forth to read their lines. They pile up together on a small table to form a picture of a stagecoach; as they look out on the imaginary scene around them the entire text is recited to us. Although crude in its form, this sight of a group of actors packed together is a strong effective image.

The final group, led enthusiastically by Roger Rees, produce a surrealist version of the text. They gather around a large piano in a grotesque parody of a genteel Victorian evening at home, and sing out to us key words and phrases from the text. A dummy baby, in the arms of Julie Peasgood, representing the "newly born", has its face suddenly ripped open to reveal gold coins (chocolate wrapped in gold foil) that are showered on us as we sit there, in a direct final assault. The politics of the passage come physically home to us, on our heads.

We realised very quickly how all this was an essential clue to a style of performance that might allow us to tackle the seemingly impossible. Whatever design we would use in the end, what we would need more than anything else was actors, actors willing to be and become the environment that they'd live and work in. The actors themselves would be our main resource. This seed of an idea with the stagecoach would be transformed later into a spectacular effect in the production, when the London stage-

The company work out how to build a stagecoach

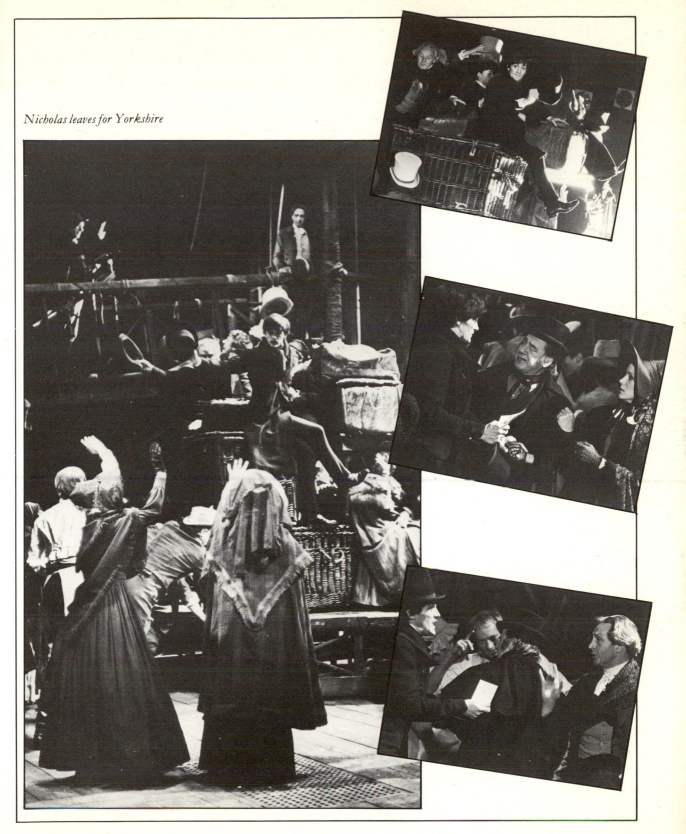

Nicholas leaves for Yorkshire

coach rattles off into the distance piled with bodies of actors.

Using their bodies and their voices to create pictures and sound, the actors had given us, as Trevor had calculated, the basis of an approach to the text in some of the difficult passages. Whatever was added later must support and not replace this basis of textual representation. As with the second story-telling exercise, involvement, attitude and personal comment by the company brought the text dynamically and dramatically alive.

The discussions that followed were of immense importance. Trevor felt that although there had been some brilliant insights and collective creations, many of the company were sceptical about this kind of work. He felt that it was important for us all to recognise the positive and negative conclusions that we could draw from what had been achieved. We had continually to indicate what was useful and could be explored further, and what had to be jettisoned on the way. To this end he introduced a new element into the discussions. This time the work would be analysed by us all with a fine critical eye. Trevor felt that he was on the line and had to demonstrate clearly that critical process under way. After a lengthy general discussion he summarised his feelings about the four versions, in particular trying to identify the problems.

Although admiring the creativity of the first group, especially the enlivening effect it had on the trapped audience, Trevor felt that particular actor/audience relationship was not one we could pursue for the Aldwych Theatre. He admired the use of sound effects (a technique that we did explore in the final production), but felt that the characteristics of the crowd of Londoners around the coach were essentially clichéd.

The second version he felt was a stunning and elegant single vision which belonged too much to the vision of one person, Edward Petherbridge. Trevor thought it excellently economical and crystalline, but almost too selective. The words were missing and the teeming, tumultuous world of London was absent with them. The conclusion seemed to be that mime was useful but only to a very limited degree.

Trevor thought that in many ways the third version was most successful, although I, and I believe most of the company, disagreed. Although agreeing that it was perhaps the least resolved of the four versions, he thought it had attacked the central question: how do you keep the nuances of Dickens's text whilst simultaneously enacting the incidents? Consequently, he found what he called this "language improvisation" to be a valuable contribution to our work.

We all discussed the final improvisation at length, accepting Trevor's definition of it as a form of agit-prop theatre. He suggested that, in effect, it had wished to abuse the audience, assail us directly, and, although exciting to watch was a very one-sided statement of what Dickens was saying. He asked the company to consider how appropriate that technique would really be to Dickens as a whole. The company generally agreed about the limitations and dangers inherent in such an approach.

By the end of the discussion the mood, Trevor felt, had changed. Although some of the company had been shocked at overt criticism, his point had been made. Having posed a question about how to communicate physically and verbally a passage from Dickens, we had analysed and concluded from the experiences learned. The process was an ongoing one of question, exercise, analysis, conclusion. Then that knowledge would be used to begin the next step.

The company were pleased by this process and eagerly awaited the next opportunity to explore, in their own way, more of these challenges.

What was also particularly thrilling during these first few days was the sight of some of the more conservative-natured actors throwing themselves into their work. It is not easy for people who have worked in a particular way for many years suddenly to throw it all away, even temporarily, and try something new. Neither directors nor actors can easily discard their old safety harnesses and touchstones. It was a fascinating experience to watch some of the highly experienced, more cautious members of the company gradually giving themselves to the work.

We now felt that another director-less piece of work should be tried. This time we gave two groups one passage from the novel, and the other two a different extract. Both exercises were completely different from the early exercise with an extract, but both still concerned journeys. The first passage is the episode in which Nicholas, just back from Portsmouth in reply to a warning letter from Newman Noggs, dashes from one address to another in London, frantically trying to discover what is happening to Kate.

The second piece, coming near the end of the novel, is a passage that explores the psychological state of the tormented, frightened Ralph Nickleby, who is near breaking point, and shows the external world through his eyes. The nightmare quality of his desperate journey is brilliantly described, but seemingly not possible to dramatise, so that again, we were beginning with the most dangerous territory. Ralph runs from house to house for his accomplices, haunted by a black cloud that seems to follow him everywhere he goes up to the moment of his suicide. This passage would take us for the first time into a non-naturalistic territory.

As before, the groups disappeared for a day and a half to their different rehearsal spaces. All over the Stratford Memorial Theatre strange noises are heard. In the balcony bar the cleaner is drawn by curiosity to the wailing sound of writhing bodies on the bar floor. The dress circle bar is evacuated by the front of house staff, who were having their coffee, as the gentle giant, Bob Peck, charges around the room in circles as though being unravelled on the end of a ball of string. In a church down the road from the theatre, the warden listens by the door to the un-christian raised voices of ten actors and actresses arguing within. The directorial team and their writer sit and have a drink. I, and maybe the others, feel somewhat left out.

Once again, late as usual, we gathered to watch the performances. The first group produced for us a version of Nicholas's journey around London. The group of actors and actresses stood in a square about ten feet by ten feet. They each represented one of the locations to which Nicholas would run. As parts of the text were narrated, Bob Peck, playing Nicholas Nickleby, began a strange series of convulsions and turns. As he whirled around and around from corner to corner of the human square, the journey of Nicholas was narrated. We were all mystified and confused. What on earth was Bob doing? In the discussions that followed, the company tried to guess the meaning of this strange performance.

"Is Nicholas meant to be ill?"

"Is Nicholas supposed to be lost?"

"Is Nicholas an epileptic?"

Finally, exasperated, Bob Peck and his group explained that they were using a symbol. What we thought was a ball of string was in fact a spider's web. Miss La Creevy and Newman Noggs had left a false trail for Nicholas to keep him temporarily out of the way. As Nicholas runs from house to house and finds no one in, he becomes more and more entangled in the web. The more he struggles (hence the erratic movements), the more he gets caught up in the web.

In their enthusiasm in trying to discover a metaphor and an original form of dramatic presentation, they, not Nicholas Nickleby, had lost their way. They had found a symbol and lost the text. Over-ingenuity for its own sake was as dangerous as a lack of imagination. The Ball of String Syndrome, as we then called it, in which a generalised (and in this case obscure) symbol takes over from specific incident and detail was a danger in all our work. In the search for a special style of production and dramatisation, we had to beware of entangling ourselves with string on the way. Trevor summarised the discussions that focused on how dangerous it was to reject Dickens's own descriptions and images in favour of an alternative. "You've not only thrown the baby out with the bath water, but the boiler and the tiles on the wall as well." "It wasn't my idea anyway," said Bob Peck.

The two versions of Ralph's journey had certain striking similarities in their use of actors to represent themselves the "black cloud" following Ralph. The actors swarmed around after their Ralph Nickleby figure, metamorphosing themselves into bodies in a graveyard or dancing, drunken figures. One group took the effect a stage further to the point where the same "black cloud" of actors became themselves the doors and walls entombing the desperate Ralph. Paddy Godfrey, veteran RSC actor, cried out in Ralph's words of despair as actors stood, coldly silent like petrified figures or statues on either side of him. In the other group, Jeffrey Dench, another of the RSC's long-serving actors, emerged as though gasping for air from a suffocating sea of bodies on the ground.

Within a few hours, new doors had been unlocked. The "Ball of String" episode was a warning to us of dangerous territory. The actors had proved that human bodies and voices could be used to create setting and invoke atmosphere whilst the actors were still acting as narrators. They could also themselves be the physical representation of nebulous and almost indefinable concepts of fear and desperation. In particular, this was an exciting possibility for the long section of the novel dealing with the events leading to the death of Ralph. Somehow we never had time to come back to that difficult section of the text until about three days before the second part of *Nicholas Nickleby* appeared to the public.

The ritual circle formed again and the microscopic examination of the work began. I believed that we were still only at the beginning of finding answers, but clearly the company felt more pleased with itself. Trevor applauded their daring and invention but felt that, on the whole, there were still not enough attempts to harness the language of Dickens to the enactment of the physical incidents. Paddy Godfrey had been perhaps the closest to this in his cries of despair when surrounded by the dumb walls of bodies.

We also discussed more general questions concerning theatre solutions as parallels or alternatives to the original text. Trevor recalled two or three productions he had seen in the USSR in which single, dominating metaphors had obscured all others. We had to try to represent all the multitudinous and varied images at work in Dickens and not select one or two to the detriment of the others.

Already, the work had moved in a new direction. As we discussed what we had done, the conversation became more and more concerned with a critique of acting and directing attitudes in general. I felt that the roots of many of my assumptions and attitudes were being explored, and I believe that many of the actors felt the same. In our search for a way to come to terms with Dickens on the stage we all had to dig away at our own preconceptions about theatre. A fascinating dialectic had begun between undramatic prose, and performer/writer/director.

At our private evening sessions Trevor had asked the all-important question: "Can we talk to the company about acting style?" If we were to open up this subject directly, the effect could be disastrous. Style is a dangerous subject for discussion as it intrudes on so many sensitive, personal areas of an actor's work. No one likes to feel that they must act in a particular way, any more than any RSC director will give a sympathetic reply if told that there is such a thing as the "Stratford style" of directing.

We agreed that it was a more general feeling about approach to characterisation that we should talk about with the company, and not specifically style as such. We had to find the reality behind the Phiz masks. As Trevor had already begun to tell the company, he believed that we should examine carefully the idea of Dickens the satirist describing his characters through a distorting lens. Phiz then drew, for the benefit of the nineteenth-century audience, those already distorted characters. What we had to do was agree on the human material that is there before the distorting satiric process begins. Then, we would have to find our own way of satirising those human beings in the theatre for an audience of our own time.

This process of going straight to the centre of character was more important than artificially trying to create a specific style. We did not have to conclude with any one way of presenting the work; on the contrary, we had to employ many different styles and techniques in order to capture and communicate Dickens's multitudinously varied work.

This focus on character that Trevor passionately described in our meetings came from the deepest centre of his beliefs about what theatre is and should be. The company should never play the effect they believe the character should make, but should play the character himself. Trevor believes that in all his work he should begin with character and then move into situation and incident. Then, an audience is involved and moved.

In this concentration on character and the human material behind character, Trevor seemed to me to be pushing toward a climax of many years of Shakespearean work at the RSC. Dickens and Shakespeare seemed to be, in an indefinable movement, beginning to merge in our work. Through the vehicle of Dickens I believe that we were moving outwards into territory concerning Shakespeare and many other theatrical works. Dickens and his array of extraordinary characters was an acting challenge of immense proportions. If the company could create these characters and make them real on the stage, without losing the humour and comments of Dickens, they would succeed in a remarkable task.

THE LIVE WRITER

*Left: Squeers (Alun Armstrong)
recaptures Smike*

David Edgar and Trevor Nunn

Soon we saw the results of another experiment. On the second day of rehearsal, in addition to their other homework, we had asked all the company to work privately for a few weeks on another exercise—an idea devised by Trevor and adapted by John Caird. Many of the early ideas were shared between them in this way. John had co-directed twice before with Trevor, on a production of *As You Like It* and *The Merry Wives of Windsor*. By the beginning of *Nicholas Nickleby* they knew each other well, and had begun to share a theatrical vocabulary. Trevor had much more experience and confidence, John, at thirty-one, still had much more to prove, but a head bursting with ingenuity and ideas. It was no more easy for him to co-direct with Trevor, a much more senior director, than it was for me to be the third member of a team that had already been working together in an intimate way. But in the early days of exploring and planning, John was always good at inventing new trials and tortures for the company to undergo.

I say torture, because for many of the company it was. We asked all the company to select a character of their choice from the novel that interested them, not necessarily one that they wanted to play. Indeed, the character did not even have to be of their own sex. They were then to present that character, alone, to the rest of us, using an extract or extracts of the character's own words from the text, in order to find their way into a particular moment in his or her life. They could use a single incident or a combination of different moments in order to show, within a couple of minutes of performance, some essential aspect of their chosen character. They were to search for the essence of their character, using Dickens's own words. They were to improvise, but without having to fake or create imaginary dialogue.

The presentations took place over the five-week trial period.

It is a nerve-wracking exercise for any actor to be asked to perform in front of his or her own colleagues. Playing to a large audience is easier and less personal, less threatening. In front of a large group of colleagues there is a strong sense of vulnerability and nakedness. However, following on from the process already begun, we believed that open criticism had to be possible among the company if true progress was to be made.

Two characters attracted the most interest: Smike and Ralph Nickleby. There were two female Smikes and two male. As each actor shuffled his or her way across the centre of the circle, some using many monosyllabic expressions of pain or fear from the text and some with almost no words at all, Smike began to come alive for us. During these few minutes Smike proved himself to be at the emotional centre of the play. It was clear that three or four of the company desperately wanted to play Smike, and although we had said that the company needn't choose a character that they wanted to play, it was easy to see why the four actors and actresses had chosen this character. We knew there would be trouble later when the final decision about casting had to be made. Ralph Nickleby created almost as fervent an interest. The burly, red-complexioned David Lloyd Meredith, another of the Welsh contingent, surprised us all by diving into the circle in a somersault to begin headfirst his account of Ralph about to hang himself—a shock effect designed to raise the level of tension. Flat on his back, as though literally crushed down by the world, he took us through Ralph's last agonising moments as he prepared the rope and thought back to his son Smike.

Roger Bizley used a sketch of a brisk Ralph Nickleby; the man of business, knocking on one door after another, using a different manner to suit each class and status of each person behind each door. Violent rudeness turned to polite smiles as he collected his debts from paupers and noblemen respectively.

Tim Brierley, one of the younger members of the company, broke all the rules. With his strong physique and curly hair, he made a strange-looking Ralph. A few minutes had been allowed for each performance, but Tim enacted an entire self-written twenty-minute play. He depicted Ralph as a skilled gambler, sitting at his desk for business as an endless stream of clients and visitors arrive. At each visit Ralph manipulates the game and the victim and turns up another card. Near the end of his life the game has gone wrong: Ralph loses control and throws in his cards and commits suicide. I felt that in Tim's piece the rich complexity of Ralph's life emerged, though Trevor felt it was an intellectual, writing achievement rather than an acting one.

Ben Kingsley, short and dark with piercing dark eyes and strong athletic body, also enacted Ralph before his moment of death, and gave us a different insight. Taking the clue from Dickens's mention of Ralph remembering his past, he added his own flashbacks of Ralph's past, building up a composite picture of fragments of Ralph from the early days of the novel. The climax came in his journey back home to kill himself when Ben knocked at the door to his attic in a strange, chilling moment as though asking permission to enter; and then there was the hanging itself. The pathos Ben extracted in his innocent portrait of a lonely, distraught man was an important aid to understanding the way Dickens was able to achieve sudden sympathy for a character who has hitherto done all he could to destroy goodness or happiness in others. The latter half of the novel becomes fascinated and obsessed with the idea of a deeply complex Ralph Nickleby, no longer in any way the villain of a melodrama, with his world in ruins around him.

Although many of the company had produced technically clever work on their chosen characters, Ben had moved into a different emotional territory. The detail and intensity of his exploration of Ralph Nickleby went beyond the simple process of character presentation into a moving and overwhelmingly serious performance. Ben demonstrated a depth of emotional commitment to his character that tore down any barriers created by fear of the nature of melodrama. Trevor quickly focused on this achievement and geared the discussion afterwards toward questions concerning our own understanding of melodrama and tragedy. The feeling that Ben's performance had been genuinely tragic forced us all to consider how our work needed to come to terms with this common Victorian mode of melodrama that might otherwise blur the true tragic centre. To this end, Trevor led the analysis through more general topics concerning Victorian tragedy and melodrama, Jacobean tragedy and contemporary attitudes to tragedy. Only through examining our preconceptions could we move towards a true understanding of how to evoke on the stage the tragic depths explored by Dickens, and felt by readers of his time.

Trevor believed that those discussions, triggered by Ben's performance, were a vital turning point in our work. Ben had proved how powerful and moving Dickens's characters could be on the stage, as long as the emotional and intellectual commitment by the actor was total.

Suzanne Bertish is the only actress I know who, on stage, can look beautiful one moment and repulsive the next without any apparent effort. From her days at Glasgow Citizens' Theatre she had learnt how to play a vast range of odd and zany characters. "I know Trevor will only want me to play grotesques anyway," she said, before the casting was decided. So, with that firmly in mind, she transformed her young body into that of an ancient hag. Choosing the extraordinary character of Peg Sliderskew, old servant to the miser Arthur Gride, Suzanne showed us a twisted, speech-slurred hag with a strong Glaswegian accent. David Edgar wrote furiously, inspired by the performance. He produced many months later a fully Glaswegian Peg, complete with "ochs" and "ayes".

When we questioned Suzanne about why she had made Peg Scottish, she said that it was simply instinct at work, based on a feeling about her name and the way she spoke. Although, perhaps, unsupportable by any textual evidence, it did give the character a full basis of reality. The motiveless, somewhat sketchy character from Dickens was now a totally believable woman. Peg seemed displaced, with her own origins lost somewhere in the distant past. Suzanne had shown how a shadowy character in the novel could be brought to life on the stage.

Two actors, David Threlfall and John Woodvine, chose the Man in Smallclothes, Dickens's endearing madman who professes passionate love arbitrarily to any female who comes near. John Woodvine erected a canvas flat in front of a platform, propping it up a few feet in the air. As we watched the flat, two legs appeared below it, gradually followed by the rest of John's not inconsiderable body. We suddenly recognised the scene in the novel when the madman appears in front of Mrs Nickleby down a chimney. Even when we had to make heavy cuts in the text months later, in an emergency last-minute attempt to rescue the audience from staying in the theatre until dawn, that scene stayed in the production. From a single short moment with a very minor character, one of the company had extracted irresistible theatrical potential.

Whilst John's achievement was technically clever, David's

Suzanne Bertish as Peg Sliderskew

*The man next door saying hallo
to Mrs Nickleby over the garden wall*

version of the same character was psychologically fascinating. Although not as funny as John's performance, David's focused on the insanity of the man. Using Dickens's own colourful language, David presented the man in smallclothes as truly deranged, and bravely tried to examine his mind.

Roger Rees poked his head between two black curtains and silently surveyed the room. Then, his face indicated that he had seen someone or something and then he disappeared again. "That's it," he said. "Have you guessed it?" We hadn't. It was, he assured us, the enigmatic figure of Brooker, the former convict who had followed Smike to Devon. Roger was enacting the scene where Brooker hides behind a tree until he sees and recognises Smike. Roger had been, in fact, the first actor to perform the exercise and had played it like a game, to break the ice.

Many other characters followed. Some performances were exquisite cameos, others were hastily conceived miscalculations that used text and incident peripheral to an understanding of character. The really successful ones were formed from the actors' own observation of some emotional truth about their chosen character.

The final offering also broke the rules. Edward Petherbridge had teamed up with the young actress Julie Peasgood, pretty and delicate as a china doll. The mime and the china doll danced together for us the dance of The Indian Savage and the Maiden. Edward, looking as always as gentle as a cat, roared ferociously like a lion and Julie trembled with fear. They danced a whole story, of the wild savage falling in love with the dancing maiden, the maiden falling asleep and then waking up to dance ecstatically with the savage, apparently as an expression of suddenly reciprocated love. Edward had choreographed the entire dance described in detail by Dickens in an episode about the Crummles Theatre Company. Edward, as Folair, the company pantomime, demonstrated beyond any doubt how much his character loathed Julie's, the Infant Phenomenon. Folair's full dislike for her reached a hilarious climax at the point when the savage had to express his love. Edward's face told the whole story.

David Edgar made a note to write it into the script.

Well, three weeks had passed, but, as yet, we had not worked on any script. Many discussions had taken place and various arguments had been debated, but it was now important to move into the next stage of work. In two weeks the trial period of rehearsal would come to an end.

The dance of The Indian Savage and The Maiden. Folair (Tim Spall) and the Infant Phenomenon (Julie Peasgood)

SCENE WORK BEGINS

There was no script yet, but David Edgar had been trying his hand at a few ideas, and he now produced four sample scenes. In his careful, analytical, organised way he had listened and watched attentively over the first few weeks. As a writer, he had the impossible job of trying to reconcile the directorial approaches so far discussed, the work already achieved by the actors and his own extensive views on what the script should be like. He also knew that from this moment on, he had to take a positive stance about the writing and demonstrate that although the work and exploration of the novel was a collective act, the actual script must come from him. Already sensitive on the subject of the writer's role, he knew he would have to move decisively and convincingly to take the initiative with the script; the politics of his position were uncertain.

David is an experienced playwright with many plays to his credit. He had also been very successful with adaptations. *The Jail Diary of Albie Sachs* was adapted from a prison diary and *Mary Barnes*, his most recent adaptation, had been drawn from a factual account of a schizophrenic's journey through madness. One of David's comments on that adaptation gives a clue to some of his particular insights that would prove invaluable later on in our work on *Nicholas Nickleby*: "Exigencies of time and clarity forced me to telescope and even alter many of the events in the book, to combine functions and people, and to find ways

John Caird suggests script modifications to David Edgar, Leon Rubin, Suzanne Bertish and Julie Peasgood

of making publicly clear what was occurring in the privacy of people's minds and souls."

With Dickens, the process would have to go a stage further to include the mind and attitude of the novelist himself. But David knew the difference between a small-scale adaptation and what we were embarking upon. All his work, with the exception of *Destiny*, which had transferred later on to a bigger stage, had been in small performing spaces, and now he was excited by the idea of a long dramatic creation for a large space. To that end he had pictures of extravagant sets and complex theatre machinery in his head. Soon he was to discover that Trevor, who had normally worked on a large scale, was imagining a bare, simple production using actors rather than stage machinery.

As agreed beforehand, David's four short scenes focused on three entirely separate social milieux. The first two scenes were set in Dotheboys Hall. The first showed Nicholas arriving to meet Mrs Squeers, and the second was the scene where Mrs Squeers feeds "brimstone and treacle" to the boys at the school. We all knew that Dotheboys Hall was potentially one of the most dramatically effective areas of the novel, and we also wanted to find out how to re-create Dickens's nightmare educational establishment without the use of children. None of the four of us wanted children in the production: but can you seriously represent a school full of boys by using adult actors?

In the third scene, work was started on Kate Nickleby's side of the plot, and the clash between money and class represented by Ralph Nickleby and Sir Mulberry Hawk. This scene was concerned with her first meeting with Lord Verisopht and Sir Mulberry Hawk at the home of her uncle. Within one short event, many key characters could be introduced. The final scene showed Nicholas arriving in Portsmouth with Smike and meeting for the first time the Crummles Theatre Company.

Four scenes and only three directors—so David Edgar was to make his debut as a director of his own work. Following our established pattern, we divided into four groups, not arbitrarily, but with a carefully organised division of actors that would allow us to see certain people in certain roles. As we went off to our separate spaces, Trevor took John, David and me to one side and whispered, "Remember, this is not a directing competition". With these words of wisdom, he went off with his group and didn't come back for two days, a day more than we had all agreed. We all had to wait for him to put exquisitely detailed final touches to his scene whilst John, David and I had had our hurried sketches finished in the agreed time. But that's

Trevor: he is incapable of a rough, hasty piece of work. His minute attention to detail and scrupulous, analytical precision has to work its own way through to a full, complete piece of work. He felt that we had underestimated the amount of time needed, and that more rehearsal was necessary to make sense of his scene.

David decided to experiment in the writing with a dramatic form that might begin to solve the problem of the narrative content of the novel. In the scene that I took, Nicholas arriving at Dotheboys Hall and meeting Mrs Squeers and Smike, David Edgar tried out his first narrative idea. As Nicholas arrives at Dotheboys Hall he suddenly speaks directly to the audience, describing his feelings:

> A host of unpleasant misgivings, which had been crowding upon Nicholas during the whole journey, thronged into his mind . . . His great distance from home and the impossibility of reaching it, except on foot, should he feel ever so anxious to return, presented itself to him in most alarming colours.

Then the dialogue between the characters continues as though nothing had been said. At various other moments during the scene Nicholas comments on the internal action directly to the audience—using the past tense as though telling the story at some time in the future:

> "The boy (Smike) put his hand to his head, as if he was making an effort to remember something, and then looking vacantly at his questioner, gradually broke into a smile."

Here, David was making the character, or the actor playing the character, into the narrator; Dickens's comment would be present throughout within the characters themselves.

This caused us endless arguments during our short rehearsal period. Should Nicholas speak directly to the audience from where he stood, or should he step out of the picture-frame of the scene and contact the audience more closely? Should he speak within character, in the voice of Nicholas, or should he speak as the actor? Should he invest the comments with the full emotional reality of the moment, or should he speak in a more detached manner, coldly and as though watching, but not necessarily feeling? Various methods were tried with varying degrees of failure. Somehow, these asides, for that is what they essentially were, seemed intrusive. David Creedon, the young actor playing Nicholas, oscillated from one idea to another as the scene progressed. We were all a little confused.

The other important part of the scene was the establishment of the character of Mrs Squeers and her relationship with Mr

Nicholas

Smike

Squeers. The scene seemed to suggest humour in their greeting of, "How is my Squeery, deary?". David Edgar, like Dickens, was trying to allow a human side to characters that could easily be seen simply as monsters. After the few hours work we had all agreed to do, we had prepared a scene of sorts. Lila Kaye, a large, outspoken, maternal actress, discovered a sharp, strong Mrs Squeers who had her husband in the palm of her hand. If there was one thing Squeers was frightened of, it was Lila's Mrs Squeers. Lila's ability to project warmth and viciousness almost at the same time started to fill out a sketchy character in the script; eventually she was cast as Mrs Squeers. But the rest of the scene moved on briskly, frustrated by confused notions of what to do with the asides. At the end, another narrative technique was used as Nicholas reads a letter from Newman Noggs, the servant of Mr Ralph Nickleby. As in many a film script, Newman Noggs was introduced directly into the scene to speak out a letter, a form of sound on vision. We brought him in quietly upstage where, as though writing at his desk, he spoke his own words as Nicholas read the letter.

After the performance there was another long discussion. No one was yet happy with the asides. Most actors believed that they interrupted the natural flow of the story. Trevor Nunn disagreed vehemently and asked to take the scene himself when we swapped round for our second attempt.

John Caird and his group produced for us the Crummles Theatre scene. The result was wildly amusing, as an endless army of eccentric characters paraded across the rehearsal room floor. Because time was so short, all the actors had looked after their own stage business as they improvised in the background. The script itself showed Nicholas and Smike being introduced to the actors. David had reintroduced the dance of the Indian Savage and the Maiden, this time accompanied by an improvised score on the piano by Roderick Horn. The overall result was delightful but totally chaotic. The focus was diffused all over the room, and the important verbal centre was completely lost. The dangers of the Crummles Theatre Company were clear. If we loved the Crummles characters and allowed too much improvisation and indulgence, the results would be fatal. The discussions afterwards were mainly about levels of credibility. Some of the characters could indeed be larger than life, but a clearer distinction had to be made between their onstage and offstage personalities.

David Edgar himself worked on the second of the Dotheboys Hall scenes. The result was stunning. Without using the large number of props needed in John Caird's version, or the furniture in mine, he offered us a simple, stark performance in an empty space. He had written another example of narrative technique, but in a different form. As each boy stepped forward from the line of boys to be fed with the foul-tasting brew of brimstone and treacle, he spoke out an instant definition of his name, his number and what he was there for. Like prison inmates, the boys had been told what their crimes were—that they were crippled, or that they were bastards, or that they were blind. It was as though this had been repeated to each of them so many times by Mr and Mrs Squeers that now that was all they knew about themselves. In David Edgar's production of the scene, the boys spoke as though they were speaking both to Mrs Squeers and to the audience. Narrative technique was thus internal and external at the same time. In the discussions that followed, many thought the boys should speak directly, in an alienated manner. But when this was eventually tried, the scene lost its impact. We discovered in this way that narrative need not necessarily intrude and could, indeed, enhance the dramatic impact of the story.

It was also clear that we could work without children. Although this line of boys looked too healthy and fit, we realised that it was only a matter of moments before the actual age of the actors became immaterial. The shock and disturbance caused by the scene could work as well with mature actors, if we approached it in a dangerous enough way. As long as we avoided

Squeers (Fulton Mackay) gives a lesson to Cobbey (John Matshikiza) and his other pupils

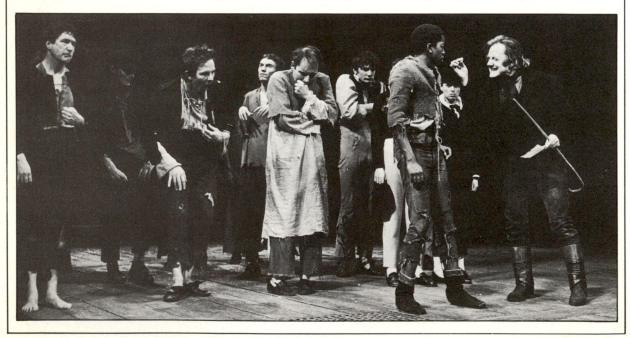

the obvious inconsistency of having the older members of the company, or anyone with a beard, amongst the boys there seemed to be no problem. And the female members of the company could blend inconspicuously with the boys with their hair pulled back off their faces. In fact, Dickens's description took on a new and chilling flavour as we watched this first look at the hapless victims of Dotheboys Hall: "Pale and haggard faces, lank and bony figures, children with the countenances of old men". What would be crucial was a total emotional and physical commitment to the acting.

The final scene was directed by Trevor. It showed Kate Nickleby being crudely teased at an all-male party at her uncle's, where she is unwittingly being used as bait to catch the rich young Lord Frederick Verisopht. At the end of the scene, she is being assaulted in another room by Sir Mulberry Hawk when interrupted by Ralph Nickleby, and the two men confront each other. This was the most successful of the scripts and was filled with detail which Trevor eagerly exploited. Both in writing and direction the scene was the first penetrating look at the aristocratic society present in *Nicholas Nickleby*. With its superficial refinement covering vulgar, greedy intentions, that world in the novel proved as rewarding to explore as the more obviously dramatic worlds of Squeers and Vincent Crummles.

Emily Richard played a quiet, ineffective Kate, uncertain and helpless, although inwardly defiant. Not through her own fault was her Kate weak and unable to defend herself. I felt that the script did not allow her a strong enough voice. As the male world of power and wealth revolved around her, her voice was totally lost. David Edgar had been true to the Dickens original —perhaps too true. Dickens, for all his brilliant insights, was still a man of his time, and does not allow his heroines much development. Many heroines of the period are sketchy, weak characters constantly rescued and protected by men. They do not often enough articulate their resistance to the evils they oppose, and are seldom shown in dynamic confrontation with them. One of David Edgar's most difficult jobs was to build up the Kate character, subtly bringing together Dickens's attitude with those of our own time. However, Trevor thought it was right to place the stress in this scene on the male conflict between Ralph and Sir Mulberry Hawk.

The rake Sir Mulberry Hawk was played with relish by Bob Peck, who demonstrated the violence hidden behind the outwardly civilised appearance, and the cool, assured manner that could at any moment turn to viciousness. And Ben Kingsley, playing a small part, upstaged all the protagonists. As the senile and loud-speaking retired Colonel Chowser, he brilliantly made the point that every role in this work was worth playing. With just a few lines he produced a dazzling sketch of a comic character that would inspire many other characterisations of parts that at first sight appeared to be unimportant.

Once again at the end of the scene, Trevor Nunn broke the rules. Having spent longer than the rest of us on his rehearsal, he also changed the script. We had agreed to direct exactly what was written on the paper, adding or changing nothing, and John and I, in our innocence, had done exactly that. Trevor reallocated lines at the end of the scene. David had experimented, as in the Dotheboys Hall scenes, with the inclusion of some narrative, and had given Ralph Nickleby a final narrative speech describing his emotions on watching his distressed niece Kate leave after the attack by Sir Mulberry. He had extracted from the book a particularly poignant description of Ralph Nickleby, in a rare moment of thoughtful sadness:

> As the door of the vehicle was roughly closed, a comb fell from Kate's hair, close at her uncle's feet; and as he picked it up and returned it into her hand, the light from a neighbouring lamp shone upon her face. The lock of hair that had escaped and curled loosely over her brow, the traces of tears yet scarcely dry, the flushed cheek, the look of sorrow, all fired some dormant train of recollection in the old man's breast; and the face of his dead brother seemed present before him, with the very look it wore on some occasion of boyish grief, of which every minute circumstance flashed upon his mind, with the distinctness of a scene of yesterday.
>
> Ralph Nickleby, who was proof against all appeals of blood and kindred—who was steeled against every tale of sorrow and distress —staggered while he looked, and reeled back into his house, as a man who had seen a spirit from some world beyond the grave.

Instead of allowing Ralph to speak the words, Trevor reallocated the speech to Alan Gill, who was playing a manservant present at the party. Alan appeared to look out of the window as though watching Ralph see Kate off. The description became his observation of Ralph. The effect was a revelation. An observer, involved in the action of the story, could tell us, like an author, what he could sense and feel coming from someone else. Ralph's psychological state could be described by an outside voice, from someone else involved peripherally in the events. The long discussions that followed came to the crux of the narrative problem. From the question raised in this scene, and the first Dotheboys Hall scene, certain conclusions emerged: wherever the author's narrative was introduced it must be as part of the events, and not separate from them; and the narrative should come from an actor in character, and not from an alienated stranger. The process seemed to work best when the emotional quality was allowed its full impact: the narrative could not be objective or emotionally distant. This seemed to be a clue in our search for our collective voice for telling a story. This early work suggested, particularly in the use of the manservant as narrator, that any character, however small, could be responsible for continuing the story. If anyone could be the storyteller, then so could everyone. Everyone on stage could be jointly and individually responsible for passing on the story.

The method of work seemed to be gradually leading us to fascinating conclusions. The process of question—experiment—criticism and analysis—rejection of wrong thinking—second experiment—conclusion was producing positive results. This theory about collective storytelling was the most exciting so far.

As a theory it was exciting, but the reality and practicality was daunting. It would mean an extraordinary responsibility for each member of the company. If they all had an obligation to continue the story, as narrators and observers, the pressure would be on them all the time. In a normal production the burden of storytelling lies with the character speaking or other characters playing in the particular scene. At other times the actor can physically, emotionally and intellectually relax. The theories that we were beginning to explore would necessitate total involvement at all times. We really would need all the company to tell all the story.

Logistically, such a process would prove to be harrowing. Every single line of narrative would have to be allocated to an appropriate actor or actress. Neither writer nor directors realised at this time the weeks and months of work ahead that these first conclusions would force us to undergo.

In the days that followed, leading up to the end of the first month's work, David tried to rewrite the scenes, reacting to the observations and criticism that had been expressed. He was not overjoyed at Trevor Nunn's reallocation of his text—it was not the way in which he was used to working—but he went to work again on his trial script.

The directors swapped over scenes, excluding David Edgar's, which had been so successful in its simplicity that none of the rest of us wanted to redirect it. Trevor took the first Dotheboys Hall scene, slightly altered to reduce the intrusion of the narrative sections. The result was agonisingly slow and detailed. Unlike the first version that I had directed, that was energetic and stressed an animated Nicholas reacting with verbal shock to his new environment, Trevor, using different actors, concentrated on building the oppressive atmosphere that surrounded Nicholas at Dotheboys Hall. Actions were slow and deliberate. The pouring of a minute brandy for Nicholas, drowned with water, and a full brandy for Squeers with just a drop of water, seemed to take an endless amount of time to achieve. As Nicholas arrived at the school for the first time, howling winds made by the actors' voices could be heard outside. Following on from David Edgar's bare stage, the furniture was minimal. The bleakness and coldness of Dotheboys Hall was powerfully created. Trevor felt, however, that the pace was not very important in an essentially unfinished piece of work. Exploring the impact of the powerful new sensations of being in a hostile environment made on the young Nicholas, he emphasised each sensation as its full weight was felt by Nicholas, and the details were exaggerated to bring a nightmare quality to the scene. Trevor seemed to direct the scene as though it was all seen through Nicholas's eyes. This then prepared us for the possibility of narrative comment directly from Nicholas to us, the audience. The short soliloquy thus becomes fundamental to the scene. Similarly, in this version, Trevor brought Newman Noggs physically into the middle of the scene, in order to speak to Nicholas the words of the letter. It was as though Nicholas had conjured up Noggs in his own mind.

Now the scene began to belong to the same world as the second Dotheboys Hall scene that David had worked on. The narrative outbursts by Nicholas were made to work much more effectively, by allowing him to speak to the audience with the same consistent emotional intensity with which he reacted within the scene as a whole. This time Nicholas spoke out to the audience, observing with anger and emotion what happened, without any physical or emotional change.

It was my task to tackle a substantially rewritten Crummles Theatre scene. In his attempt to focus the dialogue and strengthen the theatrical quality of the scene, with complex ideas of costume changing and preparation for rehearsal, David Edgar accidentally destroyed the delicate feelings he had instinctively found the first time through. The new structure of the scene was distinctly weaker than the original. In spite of this, though, this scene produced two important discussions. This time, we explored a very different feeling in Crummles's Theatre Company. At the opening the company arrived in the empty Portsmouth theatre, still carrying their luggage. As they surveyed the dark, empty, imaginary theatre, their faces all showed gloomy resignation. The reality of the tatty company, exhausted after endless weeks of touring, was true for all the actors in our company. As the cheerful actor-manager, Crummles, arrives, his optimistic, morale-boosting speeches fall on deaf ears, indifferent faces and turned backs. Nicholas meets not the cheerful eccentrics of the first version that John Caird had produced, but a group of dissatisfied and grumpy actors who all disliked each other.

John's version of the Kate scene opened with a boisterous, noisy, all-male party, with Lord Verisopht already the dupe as he drunkenly tried, presumably after a challenge, to walk across the floor on empty winebottles. As he crashed to the ground, propelled by Sir Mulberry Hawk, a bellow of male laughter was heard. This time a real party was in progress when the luckless Kate Nickleby arrived. Kate's mental torture, and her sense of female isolation in a noisy, mocking, male world, was even more painful than the first time, as the group of men all gathered closely around her, daring her to look Sir Mulberry Hawk in the eye and say that she doesn't expect to flirt with anyone at the party. Still David Edgar had not yet found a way of strengthening Kate enough and the crucial moments when Kate defies them all were blurred. Kate's inner resilience and strength had yet to be explored in order to be fully expressed. After endless discussions, these passages were rewritten and redirected many, many more times before the final production. And at the end of the scene there was a humorous miscalculation of a moment when Roger Rees mimed a manservant peeping through the curtain, watching Ralph Nickleby see Kate off, whilst Ralph said the words of narrative that were originally given to him by David Edgar. Roger distracted attention from the actor playing Ralph and the words were lost. This was an experiment to see what would happen if action and commentary were divided between two performers, and it showed us the dangers inherent in such an idea.

The hours of analysis in the circle that followed concluded that progress had been made. We had successfully invoked the bleakness of Dotheboys Hall, the truth behind the glitter of a theatre company, and the vulgarity behind the elegant clothes of the aristocrats, but some of our first instincts had been lost. The busy, complex Crummles scene was a fatal rewrite—further versions would have to be explored. The key moment of Kate's distress was still confused, whereas in the novel it was so simple and clear. We were beginning to learn how difficult the rewrit-

ing and refining process would be. However, the method of comparing and contrasting our different approaches to the work was producing dividends. Although there were still many problems, we now had a stronger direction for our future work.

The most exciting advance from these second attempts at the scenes was the success of Trevor's work on Nicholas's narrative at Dotheboys Hall. If the actor stayed in character and spoke to the audience from within the scene itself, it seemed that the narrative process did not intrude. In fact, a new quality of storytelling emerged. If that could be used, side by side with the idea of other participants in a scene watching and commenting, Dickens could be present in our work. However, how this could be applied to more complex areas of the novel remained to be seen. In David Edgar's four sample scenes, none of which was in any way yet complete, we had covered about twenty pages of a work over nine hundred pages long. We were just beginning to grasp a concept of collective narrative, but in its crude early form we had no way of knowing if we would succeed on a larger scale. The experimental work we had tried with single narrators would have to be expanded to perhaps thirty or forty actors at given points in the script. David Edgar faced the problems of working with directors who also clearly intended to be intimately involved in the scriptwriting process, whilst he himself was able for the first time to influence the direction. Our theatrical worlds seemed to be turning upside down. The actors too, having experienced an unusual degree of involvement and control in the early creative process of a production, were both exhilarated and confused. What was thrilling to some was terrifying to others. We had started to dig up old foundations but, as yet, had not fully prepared any safe alternatives.

Near the end of the fourth week, the four of us met in the evening to talk about the work so far. We all sensed the insecurities felt by the company, and knew that many actors were frustrated at having so few chances to demonstrate their ability to play certain parts. With over fifty actors and so little time, we had still almost no idea of how to cast the work. With such a small amount of script written, we did not even have enough evidence to estimate the value and importance of many key roles. Our first crisis was upon us. We had underestimated how much time the first part of our work would take. If we asked the company to make their decision in a week's time, we knew the entire work would be in jeopardy : many might leave, frustrated and disillusioned. We could not yet suggest any casting and as yet there was not enough proof that all would be well.

The next day, work on the scenes was stopped and the circle formed so that Trevor could present our case and ask for an extension. In one week it would be Christmas, the point at which, according to the original five-week timetable, all would have been decided. Trevor suggested that we should break for Christmas in a week as planned, but then continue for three weeks more in January before final decisions would be made. By then we would try our best to have the casting sorted out, but that could not be guaranteed.

After a long debate, agreement was reached. We had gained three more weeks.

LWT film David Threlfall for their documentary

The Great Debate

Before we could continue with our work, a new problem arose. Melvyn Bragg, the editor and presenter of the popular arts programme The South Bank Show for London Weekend Television, had been in contact with the RSC over an earlier programme they had done together. The South Bank Show had produced two highly successful workshops, led by Trevor Nunn and John Barton, on the work of the RSC on Shakespeare's language. Later, when editing the programmes, and talking casually about RSC plans, Trevor had mentioned *Nicholas Nickleby*. Andrew Snell, the producer and director, was intrigued, but said no more about it. Now, four weeks into the project, London Weekend Television approached us with the news that they had been given a large budget to make a special full-length feature documentary about the making of *Nicholas Nickleby*.

Trevor's first reaction was an unequivocal no. He had had bad TV experiences in the past. Once, with a camera pointing at him for an important RSC announcement about Arts Council funding, he had completely dried and his well-planned speech disintegrated. Apart from the fact that he had a deeply-rooted fear and suspicion of TV cameras, he felt that it was too late: they had already missed too much important work. However, London Weekend Television were still keen and he agreed to think more about it and consult the company.

Just after the announcement of the three weeks postponement of the trial period, he called John, David and myself together to discuss it. John was in favour of the proposed documentary, while David was, like me, cautiously in favour of their coming if certain conditions were met. We believed at that time that they would be in rehearsal with us each day, following our every movement and word, and were worried about the effect their presence would have on us and the actors, that it might interfere with and possibly destroy some of our valuable rehearsal period.

Rehearsal is a very private process. Within the four safe walls of a rehearsal room actors and directors must have the time and opportunity to allow themselves to make mistakes. They must be free to say and do stupid things, if necessary. With a television camera watching, all our instincts go towards trying to appear good-natured and intelligent and impressive all the time—the opposite to what a healthy rehearsal process is all about. No one likes to be recorded on film in moments of weakness and stress. We knew that we had already got enough problems. We feared that we would all, actors and directors, act doing a rehearsal instead of actually doing one.

However, we all shared the feeling that we were embarking on a very special project and that perhaps we should allow the process to be watched and recorded. We rarely record fully and carefully enough the work that we do. We also knew that the RSC could, in that time of financial crisis, use the extra money it would receive, and the massive publicity. We agreed, therefore, to simply present the London Weekend offer, with the arguments each way, and let the company themselves decide. As we had already been working relatively democratically, it seemed right that this major decision should be handled in the same way.

The next day we put the first couple of hours aside for discussion and decision. The discussion began at ten-thirty and continued all day and right through the evening. It became the most heated, heartfelt debate that any of us had been involved with for a long time, before and during *Nicholas Nickleby*.

Many of the company had grave doubts, fearing that the private nature of the work might be disturbed and possibly destroyed by a television presence. Others countered by arguing that because the television crew would be with us for so long we would get used to them.

Roger Rees and Bob Peck had been filmed by the same team whilst they were touring *The Three Sisters* and *Twelfth Night* for the RSC. They both spoke highly of the producer, Andrew Snell, although Bob concluded with: "You can like them, but you can't forget they're there." When someone argued that it was wrong to show to the public all the private part of our work in the theatre Roger passionately replied: "We need to show them that we're not magicians. The public must see us working and arguing and talking even if personally we may not always be seen in the best light."

As the day went on, the discussions broadened. We talked about the survival of live theatre in the future and the need to come to terms and co-operate with filmed media. We did not yet exploit mass media enough for our own benefit. A documentary that shared the excitement and the painful hours of work behind an epic work such as *Nicholas Nickleby* could only help us all in the long run. We had to balance personal fears against the overall gains for theatre as a whole.

Trevor had initiated the discussion in the belief that his personal feelings should not prevail, that a democratic process of decision was necessary, and that everyone should be able to speak, however long it took. But the only point that we could all agree upon was that we had to take a vote. Then, we could not agree how to vote! What system would be most democratic? Straight majority? Two-thirds majority? Single transfer vote?

Finally, a voting system was unanimously agreed. There would be ballot papers for every actor and each director (and after further discussion it was agreed that the stage management team should be included too). On each ballot paper there would be not two, but three options. To the question "Shall we agree to London Weekend Television coming to film us?", the

The company discuss whether London Weekend Television should be allowed to make their documentary. Left to right: John Caird, David Threlfall, Tim Spall, Willoughby Goddard, Kate Nicholls, Ben Kingsley and Julie Peasgood

answers were: 1) Yes; 2) No, but I will agree if a majority vote yes; and 3) Absolutely no. This complicated formula was to take into account every shade of opinion. Trevor insisted that even if one person voted "Absolutely no," then it must be all off. No one should be compelled to agree and no one should be compelled to leave the project. The second option was to ensure a democratic approach. Those who had reservations could indicate this but agree to go along with the feelings of the majority. If more people opted for this second clause than the first, then it was all off.

The ballot was to take place the next morning. The numerical result, to prevent any bad feeling, would be kept absolutely secret. Just yes or no would be enough. Michael Hyatt, the company manager, would act as returning officer.

Somehow, this had all become very important to the company. Through the discussions we had all had, we had talked deeply about our commitment to the work and each other in a way that we had not done before. So when Michael Hyatt came and told Trevor, John and me that the result was no, we accepted it with a deep sense of disappointment.

At least we had finally made a decision and could get on with our work, but as the day wore on, discontent spread through the company. Morale started to tumble. Whisperings of ill-feeling in the Green Room grew to direct comments expressing irritation from some members of the company.

Anger like that in theatre companies normally blows over in a day or two and in a true Chekhovian spirit work goes on. But this time it was different; it was as though the discussions had provoked thoughts and feelings about the nature of our work that would not so easily go away. Even with all this, it would, we imagined, settle again soon.

The numerical result of the ballot became known. A large majority had voted "yes". A few had said "no" but they were willing to go along with it, and one person had said absolutely "no". The veto had been used by one member of the company.

With this catalyst, the anger and upset blew up. Various individuals and small groups of actors complained to various directors and as the evening went by many wanted to find "the mole", who single-handedly had defeated the will of the company. Trevor received anguished phone calls in the early hours of the morning, begging him not to let it drop. Now, democracy was failing and the system being undermined.

In the meantime, Trevor stalled London Weekend, who were anxiously awaiting a reply, and explained some of the problems raised by the company. As a result they offered strict guarantees. Only ten days of filming, not two months as we had all so naively imagined, no cameras in the Green Room or dressing-rooms without special arrangements, and they would stop filming at specific moments if requested to do so—if it seemed that they were intruding on something very personal.

Armed with these new guarantees, Trevor called another special company meeting the next day, and now, democratic principles were discussed *ad infinitum*. Was it more democratic to go with the will of the vast majority? Another vote was agreed and this time two people voted completely against the documentary, whilst almost everyone else now voted positively for it. It was agreed to go ahead with the filming in spite of these two objections. Kate Nichols, suddenly identifying herself as one of the moles, tearfully reiterated her belief in the mistake that we were all making, but agreed to go along with the majority. The other mole declined the invitation to announce him- or herself publicly.

We awaited the arrival of the cameras after Christmas. The unidentified mole was invited by Trevor to talk privately to reach a personal arrangement. But he or she never surfaced and probably no one will ever know the mole's identity. So much for democracy.

Whilst the mole-hunting abated, the work in rehearsal continued for a few days. After a week's break before Christmas, we would have a further two weeks to complete casting and discover if the project still existed.

During those few days, we all sensed a new feeling in the company. Somehow, the long London Weekend debate had changed, intrinsically, the internal attitudes of the group. The arguing and the reflections upon our work had helped to mould a large group of fifty different actors and actresses into one single force. Many emotional statements about mutual trust and respect had been made, that made us all aware of how we would have to work collectively and as unselfishly as possible to achieve what we had in mind: many people had said how, with cameras and microphones recording our private words and thoughts, we would have to be particularly protective of each other.

It had been argued that we must allow the documentary to be made, in spite of the risk, so that we could communicate our deep belief in the importance of the work. That statement raised the consciousness of the group as to the value of what we were trying to do. The complex and elaborate system of voting had

68

been in itself an outward sign of a collective approach to a major problem. The care and understanding shown by many in these discussions towards their fellow actors, even those who held opposite views, was another sign of this moulding process at work. Morale was suddenly higher than ever before, and the destructive potential of agreeing to the London Weekend presence was for now, at least, not apparent. On the contrary, a new solidarity and collective enthusiasm had appeared.

Whilst enjoying that new confidence, we began work on another collective exercise. This was also an attempt to approach one of the difficult prose passages from different angles, before working more exclusively on the pieces written by David Edgar. We chose a fascinating piece of description that was the perfect progression for us from the previous exercises. It describes Nicholas, in a state of distress over the loss of Madeline Bray to the ugly miser Arthur Gride, wandering through the early morning streets of London. From the description of the awakening city Dickens moves into a blistering attack on all the injustices of work every day in London. From his own personal sense of having been wronged, Nicholas, as the representative of Dickens's own deep-felt opinions, externalises his sense of injustice to include others in the city around him. From the earlier juxtaposition of "poverty and wealth" in the earlier passage about London, Dickens progresses in this piece to a direct attack and comment on the way of the world.

> But now, when he thought how regularly things went on from day to day in the same unvarying round—how youth and beauty died, and ugly griping age lived tottering on—how crafty avarice grew rich, and manly honest hearts were poor and sad—how few they were who tenanted the stately houses, and how many those who lay in noisome pens, or rose each day and laid them down at night, and lived and died, father and son, mother and child, race upon race, and generation upon generation, without a home to shelter them or the energies of one single man directed to their aid—how in seeking, not a luxurious and splendid life, but the bare means of a most wretched and inadequate subsistence, there were women and children in that one town, divided into classes, numbered and estimated as regularly as the noble families and folks of great degree, and reared from infancy to drive most criminal and dreadful trades— how ignorance was punished and never taught—how jail-door gaped and gallows loomed for thousands urged towards them by circumstances darkly curtaining their very cradles' heads, and but for which they might have earned their honest bread and lived in peace—how many who could scarcely go astray, be they vicious as they would, turned haughtily from the crushed and stricken wretch who could scarce do otherwise, and who would have been a greater

wonder had he or she done well, than even they, had they done ill—how much injustice, and misery, and wrong there was, and yet how the world rolled on from year to year, alike careless and indifferent, and no man seeking to remedy or redress it:—when he thought of all this, and selected from the mass the one slight case on which his thoughts were bent, he felt indeed there was little ground for hope, and little cause or reason why it should not form an atom in the huge aggregate of distress and sorrow, and add one small and unimportant unit to swell the great amount.

Newman Noggs bids farewell to Nicholas and Smike

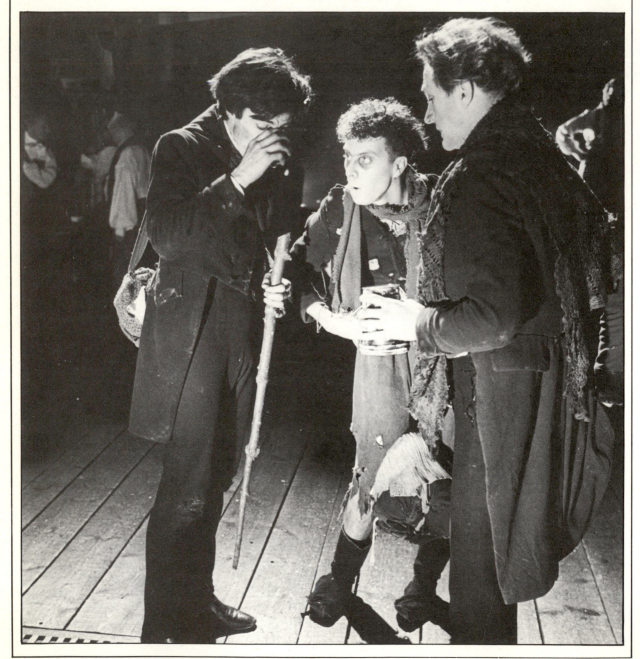

Paddy Godfrey

Bill Maxwell, Alan Gill and Julie Peasgood as narrators

Dickens is here at his most angry and most specific; he is also writing in his most theatrically undramatic style. This final prose extract was the most important expression of Dickens the moralist, the journalist and the political commentator, and was also the most elusive as far as a dramatisation was concerned.

The company was divided into four groups and went off to prepare their own versions of the passage. A few days before the Christmas break, we saw the results. This time, the versions were surprisingly similar. At last we were beginning to share a theatrical language. All the groups used selected passages from the text, divided among different narrators, and used the basic idea of a thronging crowd of people in London. There were also the rudiments of improvised characters and minute internal scenarios between them. On the whole, however, what emerged was a noisy, bustling crowd of anonymous Londoners, suddenly speaking out their allotted extract from Dickens's text. The specificity and intensity of anger was blurred, although the basic approaches to the text were clearly well conceived. The chaos that resulted was thrilling to watch as each group enthusiastically turned Dickens's prose into a dramatic scene of London street life.

This time, the discussions turned to the questions of style that we had so far avoided bringing up directly. Trevor bravely offered to try a new exercise himself, to provide some answers. He decided to attempt something we had not done before: he would take all four versions of the passage and by cutting and changing and specific direction, try to form a composite final version.

Until then, we had deliberately left all previous exercises in their rough, unfinished state, in order to come back to them much later when ideas were more carefully formulated. Trevor believed that in the little time that we had left before the end of our eight-week period of trial, we had to demonstrate a positive result from the experimental exercises. Otherwise it would seem as though we always hurried on to the next piece of work leaving questions unanswered. To channel the new collective energy and harmony that we all felt, he believed that at least this, possibly the individually most important passage in the novel as far as we were concerned, should be pursued to as close a final form as we could at that moment possibly conceive. At the same time it would raise some of the key stylistic questions about collective storytelling that we had toyed with for the first month of work. He began the process of combing the four versions that same afternoon, intending to continue the exercise after the

Christmas break.

Meanwhile, for the last two days' work before Christmas, we had a little work to finish on David's first scenes. Trevor, in particular, wished to work more on the Squeers scene. But on Christmas Eve Trevor had to dash away from rehearsal. When we met him later he looked tired and pale. His house had just burnt down.

His Stratford home had been destroyed by a fire caused by a short-circuit. What was even worse than the fire damage was the destruction caused by the water used to put it out. His office, in which the four of us met each night, was turned into a temporary refugee camp with stereo system, records, books and clothes lining the floors and chairs.

For the last few hours before Christmas, work had to go on; we had one more piece of work to introduce. We had always felt that music would be an essential, integral part of our work. We did not yet know what shape or form it would take, but there would be, we were sure, a lot of it. Before the break, we wanted to add that element in some way to our work. For one thing, singing is another way of bringing a group of people close together. So, organised by John, whose musical talents clearly made him the best qualified, and aided by Roderick Horn, the company rehearsed for a few hours the Christmas carol "The Holly and the Ivy". Trevor and I joined them later in the day to hear the result. The sound was surprisingly good and we realised immediately that there was much singing talent in the group. Together, the company sang the carol with an energy and joy that compensated for some of the less musically proficient contributions. But that was exactly the intention behind it: to unleash the immense power of a large company singing. We knew that we would have to explore that sound later in our work. The emotional impact would be as important as the more cerebral, verbal contributions that we had already heard.

It was no accident that we chose a Christmas carol for our first musical exercise; and it was not simply the topical timing of the event.

In our earlier conversations about Dickens, Christmas had often been mentioned as the trigger for many memories. In all our minds there is a close connection between Christmas and Dickens; it is often said that Dickens made Christmas, at least Christmas in the English tradition that we now think of. As Conor Cruise O'Brien wrote in his *Observer* column on 23 December 1979: "The kind of Christmas we celebrate is more a Dickensian than a purely Christian heritage, with its combination of generous sentiments towards the poor and weak, with over-spending, over-eating, over-drinking, and over-thinking".

It is true that our Christmas associations of goodwill to our fellow men are part of our Dickensian inheritance. As that article went on to say, Dickens's basic sentiment is that the world would be a better place if it were Christmas 365 days of the year. Dickens fights not just against individual problems but against injustice and inhumanity in whatever form it takes.

Our discussions progressed from this article to an essay on Dickens by George Orwell, who says that this feeling that Dickens embodies, that men should behave better with each other, is not as naive as it seems. It is not the shape of society that needs changing, but the attitudes of men themselves. Therefore, he concludes, Dickens ultimately rises above many apparently more radical writers and thinkers in his attacks on injustice and inhumanity, when they are simply fighting for specific causes and politics: or as Orwell describes it, "the smelly little orthodoxies which are now contending for our souls".

This led us to a discussion about the radical nature of Dickens's writings. Is he really radical, or does he jump on the bandwagon of causes that are already being fought? Articles about the notorious Yorkshire schools had appeared in the newspapers before *Nicholas Nickleby* was written. Conor Cruise O'Brien, in the same *Observer* article, claims that "the social impact of Dickens's writing has been very great, and greater in *relation to Britain*, than of Marx himself". We were dubious about this claim, but the point was still made: Dickens has had a profound effect on social attitudes in this country. Karl Marx was also an admirer of Dickens and believed in his importance in the fight against injustice.

However, as Orwell too agrees, Dickens is undeniably middle-class in his attitudes. He has a fondness for those whom he mocks. His own life reflected some of those contradictions. He ended up as a complete English middle-class gentleman, owning valuable property and land. He believes in the middle classes, but wants to make them better people. The Cheerybles are the epitome of this process at work.

All this is why Christmas was so important for our work. It relates to all Dickens's work as well as *Nicholas Nickleby* in particular. Although not specifically located at Christmas in the novel, the movements at the end of *Nicholas Nickleby* are toward a harmony, celebration and reconciliation that is in many ways what we think of as a Dickensian Christmas. The progression through the novel from the bleak winter coldness of Yorkshire

Andrew Smell, director,
South Bank Show, LWT

and Dotheboys Hall, through seasonal cycles to another final warm and safe winter, inside happy homes, was appropriately close to a Christmas celebration. Yet the ever-present and lingering memories of Smike and Dotheboys Hall are never quite fully melted by the warmth. And Dickens ends the novel with a reference to Smike's grave. We believed that in some way Christmas might be the right way to end the dramatic adaptation, enabling us to explore the reconciliation and harmony but also, more importantly, the contradictions and unfinished stories of misery. We hoped it would be possible in some way to celebrate the end of Dickens's, Nicholas's, and our own epic journey, and come to terms with the still angry Dickens. It was only later in our work that David Edgar suggested a practical and brilliant way of achieving that end.

For now, collective singing was a way of drawing the company together before the break and of bringing music into our work. The singing ended and Christmas began.

THE NEW YEAR

Mr and Madame Mantalini at breakfast

1980 began. Before the company gathered together to begin the final two weeks of experimental work, Trevor, John and I met to review our position.

We were still not at all sure how to cast the play. Oddly, only one or two pieces of casting seemed now to be obvious; well over 90 per cent was completely undecided. We agreed to move into top gear. We still had to work through another three scenes already prepared by David Edgar, and Trevor had to explore further his ideas on "London at Dawn". There were certain actors we wanted to watch in certain roles, but during all this work we would also have to give as many people as possible a chance to play characters they were interested in. London Weekend would be arriving in a few days and work might consequently slow down. And, most of all, we wanted to find out how the play might begin and experiment with the proposed opening that David Edgar, who had gone back to the USA for some days, had left us, along with two other scenes.

Reviewing all this we had a strong feeling, again, of time running out. Trevor raised the issue that had been on all our minds. When the project had first been conceived, the plan had been to rehearse in Stratford, then for four weeks in Newcastle, before bringing the work to London in order to open the London season in April 1980. We had not even more than scantily rehearsed a few short scenes out of what might be a total of about a hundred. We knew that the schedule would have to be put back at least a few weeks and probably longer. We had already spent the equivalent time on *Nicholas Nickleby* to almost an entire normal Shakespearean production rehearsal period. We were also concerned about the morale effect of any postponement. So, we left the date open for Trevor to negotiate in relation to all the other problems coming in London in the spring.

At this time, the work was still shapeless. We knew it would by necessity be longer than a normal three-hour production, but more than that we had no way of knowing. It might be one very long evening, or two or three or more. If we really were going to attempt the whole novel, whatever we ended up with would be very, very long. We agreed that this structural question must be decided soon to enable realistic planning in the spring.

When we gathered again we were without two of the group: our first two casualties. Ian McNeice had left the project for personal reasons; he had other problems to work out and *Nicholas Nickleby* already did not leave anyone much time for anything beyond itself. We also lost Donna Champion who, disillusioned with working in a big company, wanted to leave the RSC completely in order to return to fringe theatre work.

So, with our slightly depleted group, we continued work moulding together the four early versions of "London at Dawn". The company analysed these exercises with Trevor. He wanted to root the work firmly on the text. We had still not yet succeeded in physicalising a piece of Dickens's text and using his words at the same time. Trevor wanted to go back to Dickens's description of the city coming gradually to life. He also reminded the company that the most successful work so far had been in their commitment to character. The text had been more vibrant and alive when spoken in character. Few precise ideas of profession, class or character had been worked on in the first versions of this extract. Trevor wanted to focus, as had Dickens in the original passage, on the poor of London.

After a discussion about what people might be seen at dawn in 1830s London, some actors and actresses fixed on their professions. Three actresses elected to be poor women scrubbing away outside the front door as housemaids at their first duty of the day. Other actresses elected to be whores (accustomed to the role after many such parts in RSC productions), or milliners on their way to work. Actors opted for gaslight-men putting out the street lights, road-cleaners, pickpockets, street-vendors, blind beggars, hurdygurdy-men, pimps and aristocrats. The research papers on Victorian England were clearly still fresh in everybody's minds. When everyone had fixed on a profession they were then to begin work on a character within that class and occupational framework. The company were then asked to improvise the scene again together.

Trevor let the improvisation run for over twenty minutes, at the end of which anarchy ruled. The strain of a long improvisation with characters still fresh in everyone's minds was too great. Pickpockets ran noisily back and forth stealing everything in sight, and the hurdygurdy-man sang loudly, drowning other people's words. Whores solicited trade from customers who were being harangued by blind and lame beggers. Babies were heard crying and milliners conversed in loud voices whilst dogs barked in the background. In the midst of the clamour and bustle a fight broke out between two poor-looking women, Cathryn Harrison and Julie Peasgood. They rolled around on the floor biting and scratching each other whilst a crowd gathered to watch.

In the most free improvisation yet attempted, chaos reigned. But within that undisciplined frenzy a vast amount of invention was released.

The next stage was to select and refine the material. This time everything would be sequential. Trevor began to construct one precise moment after another in pictures and sound, to suggest the awakening city.

He then went on to an even more refined third version of the scene, that for the first time was fully structured. This time it all took place in only a few minutes, centred around a compressed known order of events. By now all confusions of identity were avoided as everyone knew what each other's functions were.

First we hear the sound of the hissing gaslights, made by three or four actors. A lonely figure moves across the floor, carrying a pole, and mimes putting out the lights one by one. The hissing cuts out in time to his movements. A solitary dog is heard barking in the distance. Three tattered women arrive one after another and start scrubbing front doorsteps. Sounds of activity float into the picture as other London characters start to appear. Horses are heard passing by, their reins rattling. Two milliners walk hurriedly by on their way to work and cross the road by a sweeper who is languidly going about his work. Voices of street vendors are heard selling their wares. Each sound and movement is precisely orchestrated and synchronised into a continuous movement from dawn to early morning. One or two of the early morning street vendors appear, selling food. Two gents pass by on their way home, still dressed up from the party the night before. As the morning moves on, the street comes more and more to life with the gradually increasing bustle and energy of the day. The overall effect is of a slowly-building climax; a smouldering, slow-burning fuse getting closer to its explosion point. As the noise and crowd swell, pickpockets and whores join the proceedings. Suddenly, the noise reaches a pitch and the characters suddenly turn towards the audience as the actors come to the point in Dickens's narrative when his anger is expressed in Nicholas's thoughts about London.

Now the company all sit down in a circle again, and Trevor allocates specific lines to each person, using selected parts of the text. The first lines go to individuals, but as the sequence goes on some lines are given to two or three actors at the same time. This process is slowly increased until three lines are shouted out by first part of the company and finally all of them together. The cry of "inadequate subsistence" is repeated by the poor people of London as the build-up to a climax of anger against all the injustices that take place in the city. As they enact it again, with the text, Nicholas joins in. He sees all the angry faces around him and physically they swallow him up into the middle of the crowd as his conclusions about his own misery begin: "He felt indeed that there was little ground for hope and little cause or reason why it should not form an atom in the huge aggregate of distress and sorrow, and add one small and unimportant unit to swell the great amount." Nicholas's personal pains are merged into those of all the people of London around him.

In his minutely analysed picture of the awakening London Trevor had made a major statement about style. We had already demonstrated in the earlier work that each actor could narrate the story in or out of character, using the first and third person at the same time. We had also shown that anyone and, indeed, everyone could act as a narrator. We had seen how important it was to use the actual text; pictorial representations alone were not enough to express the subtle textures and tones of the original. Now, after a process of experimentation, scrutiny, criticism, further experimentation and structuring, Trevor had merged all these different elements. He had also experimented with collective speaking. This time, the entire company had come to terms with a section of narration. Significantly, it had been with a passage from Dickens that was centred on anger. In Trevor's version of the scene, the people of London themselves seemed to be crying out in helpless fury.

The end result was our first true success in coming to terms with the area of Dickens normally lost in adaptations. A long discussion about style now took place and this time resulted in a formula we could more or less agree on, although John did not believe that what Trevor had done with the collective speaking really worked. It had already been clear that the strength of narrative comment came from a basis in character and emotional involvement in the scene. What was new in Trevor's work was a collective voice speaking, first a few voices and then all of them, but John was not happy. He claimed that actors speaking together are "dehumanised". He felt that by speaking in the same rhythms together, they lost the force of the emotion. "Commitment is impossible in this way of speaking," he said. Later, he also objected to the Cockney accents used by the low-life characters and the poor: "Middle-class actors speaking in working-class voices a literate writer's words". John wanted to try the scene without false accents and with a single voice for each line. His version was tried at a later date, against Trevor's better judgement. In fact, the power of collective anger was lost when single voices cried out, and the characters of the poor seemed even more contradictory when middle-class accents were used. Eventually, months later, a compromise was found in a slightly modified version of what Trevor had now produced. The edges of the accents were slightly softened and some of the choral speaking was taken out, but the climactic litany of voices near the end stayed the same.

A way of collective storytelling that did not intrude on the internal movement of plot, character and incident was beginning to emerge. Trevor took the scene that had been written down, and altered and cut the words to produce a fully rhythmic script, almost like a musical score, to facilitate an improved reading of key words and phrases.

Our only regret was that London Weekend had not been there to film it all. We all felt it had been one of our most important moments and that there might not be many more as good.

We then progressed quickly to the next three scenes David had left us to work on in his absence in the USA. Two of the scenes concerned the activities of Mr and Mrs Mantalini, the owners of the millinery establishment to which Kate Nickleby is first sent to work by her uncle Ralph.

The first scene, directed by me, is the first introduction of Kate to the Mantalinis, where she accidentally overhears their breakfast conversation. Embarrassed by the arguments and the excessive endearments expressed by Mr Mantalini, she coughs to attract their attention. She is briefly interviewed for the job, while Mr Mantalini flirts with her outrageously. The verbally inventive Mr Mantalini was played by John McEnery, who quickly discovered the delights of the part. The breakfast scene was hilarious as the row about his over-expenditure was suddenly transformed into a momentary love scene, and then back to a discussion about cash. We knew that Dickens had given us another brilliant eccentric creation that could be brought to life.

Above: Mr and Mrs Mantalini meet Kate Nickleby (Emily Richard) for the first time

Top left: Madame Mantalini introduces Kate Nickleby (Susan Littler) to Miss Knag and the milliners

Left: Kate (Emily Richard) at the Mantalinis

Bottom left: Janet Dale as Miss Knag

Mantalini is a real phoney!

The dialogue given to Kate Nickleby was becoming stronger. Her gentle but firm rebuff of Mr Mantalini's advances was gradually beginning to get closer to our conception of a strong heroine. Although David Edgar had written Ralph into the scene, accompanying Kate to her first interview, we found in rehearsal that it was better with her alone; she then becomes more vulnerable, and consequently stronger when she demonstrates her ability to cope with a difficult situation.

What was missing from it all was a true sense of the seriousness of the dangers present to Kate at the Mantalini establishment. Mr Mantalini was so successful as a comic creation that the threat to Kate was not strong enough. I believed that in some way Dickens was setting up a situation for Kate parallel to that of Nicholas at Dotheboys Hall. Although not so viciously cruel and bleak an environment as Dotheboys Hall, the millinery establishment was nonetheless a dangerous territory for a young innocent girl, who had never worked away from home before. Some of our research had shown that milliners were often exploited and ill-treated, and one historical source had even suggested that they were so badly paid that they often turned to prostitution to supplement their meagre wages.

We turned to the novel for further evidence and, sure enough, there were ominous references to Kate's plight.

> At this early hour many sickly girls, whose business, like that of the poor worm, is to produce with patient toil the finery that bedecks the thoughtless and luxurious, traverse our streets, making towards the scene of their daily labour, and catching, as if by stealth, in their hurried walk, the only gasp of wholesome air and glimpse of sunlight which cheers their monotonous existence during the long train of hours that make a working day. As she drew nigh to the more fashionable quarter of the town, Kate marked many of this class as they passed by, hurrying like herself to their painful occupation, and saw, in their unhealthy looks and feeble gait, but too clear an evidence that her misgivings were not wholly groundless.

Clearly, there was a knowledge of dressmakers and milliners available to Dickens's readership that was crucial to their understanding of what Kate was entering into. Therefore, using the narrative technique as a means of creating an atmosphere and expanding our own present-day knowledge of the situation, we added it as a form of prelude to the scene. Kate spoke those lines on her way to the Mantalinis. Later, they were transferred to the other girls walking by.

It was Trevor who directed the second Mantalini scene, set in the milliners' workshop. The first part of the scene deals with Kate Nickleby's first meeting with Miss Knag, the head assistant to Mrs Mantalini, and the other milliners. In the second half of the scene a rich lady and her daughter come to buy hats and the luckless Kate gets in the way while trying to serve them.

Trevor seemed to have two main objectives in his work on the scene. The first was to push further the idea of internal storytelling narrative from minor characters, and the second was to introduce music directly into a scene for the first time. He set the scene around a long table with the milliners sitting next to each other, stitching and cutting. In character, as young working girls, each with her own distinct personality, the milliners, facing the audience, comment with humour and a point of view on the events taking place on the stage. Instant character sketches brought them to life as they busily sewed and glanced up to communicate information to us. Again, the effect was simple, successful, and not intrusive.

In the second half of the scene, whilst Kate is attending the difficult customers, Trevor switched on a tape of Handel's "Water Music". The grandness and sense of occasion produced by the music was intended as an apparently satirical accompaniment to the mime of Kate hopelessly trying to fit a hat on the rich daughter. The elegance and grandeur of the mime, music and costume hit at the centre of Dickens's social satire in the scene. In performance, Trevor's carefully organised sequence of events collapsed. Speeches overlapped and the music and mime sequence were not synchronised. In spite of this the basic concept came through, and Trevor offered to work again for a day or two on the scene to try and organise it more carefully. Although the musical satire had not been very successful in itself, it did awaken possibilities for other points in the play.

The third scene, concerning the opening to the play, was to cause us more problems than anything hitherto.

Having learned some of the rules that would guide us through the work, we felt it would be good physically and psychologically to plan the beginning. Whatever theatrical language would be used throughout must in some way be indicated and introduced at the opening to the work.

The novel has, in effect, two openings. First, there is a short history of the Nickleby family tracing the events leading to the death of Nicholas's father, and the consequent journey of Nicholas, Kate and Mrs Nickleby to London in order to seek aid from the dead man's brother, Ralph Nickleby. Then, having used this family narrative as a form of prelude, Dickens begins the story over again with the business background of Ralph Nickleby. After introducing to the reader Ralph and his clerk Newman Noggs, he launches into an extravagant, colourful and highly satirical account of the corrupt gang of businessmen, politicians and clergy forming the United Metropolitan Improved Hot Muffin and Crumpet Baking and Punctual Delivery Company. With this device the reader is immediately aware of the nature of Ralph's business practices, before Dickens brings Ralph's world together with Mrs Nickleby's and her family's.

David felt that it was crucial for the muffin company scene to be in the script. In any other adaptation there would never be room for such an incident. As he said in an interview with London Weekend: "I want it because the plot is about money and the main plot of the book is almost all about money and rela-

Top: The full company speaking the opening narration to the play

Centre and bottom: The company becoming the people of London

tions between people and their money and I wanted to start with a scene about money". Theatrically, he wanted to begin with a strong statement about Ralph Nickleby and his involvement with money, because Ralph carries the main burden of the financial plot. Therefore, unlike Dickens, David wrote a draft scene that began with the meeting of the muffin company.

For David it was a way of beginning with a surprise. Throwing the audience straight into a bustling meeting about the incorporation of a company would be a shock to them, warning that the work in front of them was not in any way a traditional Dickens adaptation. He decided that his one scene should include both the Dickens openings of the first three chapters, beginning with the company and then moving backwards and forwards between that and the narration of the family history and Nicholas's and Kate's and Mrs Nickleby's arrival in London.

David was still in the USA when the scene, which John Caird directed, was shown to the rest of us. It confused us all, and the actors in it were unhappy. The complex problems of the meeting itself were bewildering. It was not clear who the crowd present at the meeting represented; it was not even obvious that a confidence trick was taking place. The narrative sequences concerning the Nickleby family broke up and destroyed the continuity of the company scene. Although effective as an idea, the script seemed to confuse and blur the issues. In the enactment there was also a problem. The characters of Mrs Nickleby, Kate and Nicholas were introduced by one actor and performed by another, according to Edward Petherbridge, as "cardboard cutouts". The crowd was staged in a way that seemed to add to the problems. John Caird, grappling with the most difficult script so far, in a brave attempt to solve the ever-present stage problems of a small group of actors pretending to be a huge mass, had introduced a form of split-screen device. The crowd were placed upstage facing the audience, but everyone else in the scene played towards the audience as though they themselves were the crowd. Before, the actions and noises made by the crowd upstage were reacted to by Ralph Nickleby and his fellow company directors as though coming from us, the audience. Unfortunately this ingenuity added to the problems already present in the script and caused complete chaos. The loud and boisterous crowd seemed more like a fixed rent-a-mob or football crowd than potential middle-class investors. In both script and performance there was a continual confusion between the different interest groups and crowds represented: the directors, the potential investors and the muffin-boys.

In the usual long discussion, many criticisms emerged. John proposed that he and I should rehearse an alternative version to the scene. As David was not there to comment, defend or re-write, we felt it only fair to present both versions to him on his return in a few days. Our idea was to begin, like Dickens, with the family history and then move on to the muffin scene, keeping the two scenes separate. John took on the task of trying to re-work the muffin scene whilst clarifying all the areas of confusion within the script. I agreed to try and experiment with the family history to try and find a theatrical way to tell it.

The next day, work on the rerehearsing of those scenes began. Trevor was particularly happy to be reworking the Mantalini scene in the Dress Circle bar, because it turned out to be Day One for London Weekend Television. They installed their cameras in the Conference Hall where the larger group was re-hearsing with John. As expected, the first presence of the cameras produced an uneasy rehearsal for John, whilst Trevor was busy and happy upstairs. The problems in all the work were more complex than we planned and rehearsals continued for two more days. Just as we felt we were almost ready to show again the scenes to each other another problem arose. Trevor became ill. In agony, he had to go home to his temporary flat in Stratford; his house had of course been burnt down a few weeks earlier. It was the evening of 14 January, his fortieth birthday.

With Trevor in bed, the next day, diagnosed as having an acute attack of fibrositis, John and I continued the work on the opening scene.

John battled through all the problems inherent in the muffin company meeting, clarifying the blurred moments and establish-ing correct public meeting procedure for amendments and votes. He also restaged the crowd facing the stage, as part of the audience. Interruptions and complaints would now come directly from where the rest of us were sitting. On the stage area he placed a large group of company directors who would all take part in the ensuing pageant. The patriotic and financial speeches were now made directly to the audience, and the crowd re-sponded not as football supporters but as the respectable middle classes. The muffin-boys stood separately and were clearly identi-fied as angry victims trying to disrupt the meeting. Two police-men were present, one of them in the burly shape of Bob Peck, to keep law and order.

Meanwhile, I worked with about fifteen actors on trying to tell the opening story. This time I asked them to try and tell the tale with joy and humour instead of earnestness. The lines were

The sequence continues

divided up, not just between a couple of narrators but the entire group. The actors representing the Nickleby family would begin as part of the group of actors but eventually emerge and move to a central position in character, speaking their own lines from the text. When a farm was mentioned, animal noises were made; when Nicholas and Kate are described as children, childlike singing could be heard; when money is mentioned large pieces of white paper change hands; when a wedding is mentioned the same paper is torn to shreds and used as confetti. A group of actors and actresses would very simply enjoy the sharing of a story that collectively they wanted to impart to others, in a simple, joyous form of collective storytelling.

John and I spent a morning moulding the two scenes together, and in the afternoon we watched it right through. The result was a very much more lucid account of the first three chapters of the novel. The storytelling lifted it all off to a humorous start and the company scene was not easy to follow. But when David Edgar came back a couple of days later and saw the two versions he was not as happy as John and I. He still believed that his original version was "more dramatic" and more unusual and exciting. Many days passed before the answer was found and David, eventually agreeing to the basic new structure, then brilliantly transformed the crude reworking that John and I had done into a scene close in spirit to his original intention. He re-introduced some of the original satire cut out by John, until the final scene represented both attitudes. Trevor then redirected the scene, many weeks later in London, and modified it further. He staged the meeting directly toward the audience, with muffin-boys actually among the public in the auditorium. He also simplified the first narrative section until all mime had been taken out. The spirit remained the same, but it was transformed into a purely vocal storytelling sequence. It was the first time that all three directors and writer had been involved in the creating of a scene.

London Weekend Television eagerly followed all these rehearsals and discussions as their first insight as to what *Nicholas Nickleby* was all about.

The cloud over it all was Trevor's illness. Whilst John and I were reworking the first scene, Trevor was still ill. "While the cat's away . . .," observed Edward Petherbridge. We had now reached the end of our eight-week deadline and had to announce casting if the project was to survive. With Trevor ill in bed we now had the biggest problems yet in the project.

END OF TERM

Trevor Nunn directing at the Rainbow Theatre

The day after his fortieth birthday, Trevor Nunn lay in bed, still in great pain. The strain of those first few weeks had taken their toll. With the intense personal commitment necessary for the type of work we were doing, and performances every night after an entire season of productions, the whole company were very tired. Many actors had fallen ill in the weeks before Christmas. Now it was Trevor's turn.

It was perhaps not totally coincidental that Trevor had become ill on the evening of his birthday. Even though he looks years younger than he really is, he had been joking for some days about getting old and about the psychological barrier of leaving his thirties.

Trevor has been Artistic Director of the Royal Shakespeare Company since the age of twenty-seven, and he was an assistant director before that. He had worked on one production after another. Rarely in those years had he been ill—though, as I realised more and more from working beside him, running an organisation the size of the RSC is itself a full-time job.

Trevor Nunn is an extraordinary man. He juggles daily with the lives of a vast number of people directly or indirectly involved with the Royal Shakespeare Company. Although he now shares the burden of being Artistic Director with Terry Hands, he did to a large extent personally steer the RSC through several times of crisis. The cautious and persuasive personality that allows

David Threlfall asks Trevor Nunn and John Caird for advice

him to have kept an enormous, complex company like the RSC afloat for so many years was the guiding force behind *Nicholas Nickleby*. Many of the acting company are dedicated to Trevor and his frequently brilliant work, and without their absolute trust and confidence in him the production could never have begun or gone so far. Now, at a crucial time in our work, he was away from the theatre and had to continue his meetings with John and sometimes with me in the bland and sterile environment of his temporary "modern luxury flat" in Stratford. We were all most upset to see the pain he was in with what was later realised to be a severe locking of the neck muscles and strained tendons, caused by lack of rest and overwork.

In *Nicholas Nickleby*, Trevor was departing from many of his old ways. Responsibility for the production was already being shared among the whole company. (Much later in the rehearsal period, Trevor would occasionally become irritated by "direction by committee".) It was one of the few times in all his directing career that he had worked with a live author. He was used to interpreting and modifying scripts as he saw fit. David Edgar was, however, alive and more than willing to kick. Moreover, it was the first time that Trevor had embarked on a project without a written script. For many years he had avoided new plays because he so often found himself out of sympathy with the material. He felt that more fulfilling work could be done on texts that make great demands; scripts that offered no possibility of letting him down. It was then he who had to ensure that he did not let them down. Similarly, the nebulous world of adaptations and lengthy improvisations was relatively alien to him.

Trevor is not a man to delegate unless he has to. In spite of the existence of a group of skilled administrators at the RSC, he has always made many decisions on his own, at least until the sharing of the Artistic Directorship with Terry Hands began. A brilliant administrator and experienced politician, he hates to have his back against the wall and lose control of a situation. He throws as many balls into the air at the same time as possible and keeps them there until he must choose which to catch. He carefully analyses and persistently holds on to every possibility as long as he can before making any decision. When directly confronted with unpleasant requests or accusations his deeply-set eyelids lower and his normally attentive eyes turn away to the ground. He dislikes being rushed or pushed into decisions of any kind. When Trevor, John Caird and I walked through the crowded streets of Covent Garden between rehearsals, John and I would

Trevor Nunn directs Nicholas and the Crummles children

always have crossed through the moving traffic to the other side before him—although Trevor puts that down to his inability to judge the speed of a moving object.

Trevor had great faith in John Caird—their close and trusted friendship was a bond at the centre of our work—so when Trevor went sick John and I continued as best we could in his absence. The greatest problem was the casting. If there was one area in which Trevor's experience and abilities were essential, it was in this delicate area of the diplomatic and artistic balancing act of casting. Just before his illness Trevor and John, aided by David and me, had begun to formulate a skeleton plan for casting. Certain basic factors had seemed clear. There were not enough parts to satisfy all the male members of the company. When the project had begun, it had seemed as though there would be plenty for everyone, but now, after a very specific breakdown of the script, it was not quite so. Having taken the tentative decision that the play would be in two parts, to be performed on separate evenings (although we still reserved for ourselves the right to change this decision), we could fairly accurately gauge the major doubling problems, and could see that there would be a shortage of male parts. There could be something for everyone, but never enough to please or satisfy all.

Ironically, there were not enough actresses to play all the female roles. Having already lost one female, we already knew that outside actresses would have to be brought in. Along with the male casting problem, it was a potential time-bomb. After eight weeks of intensive, difficult work there would be immense resentment of outsiders. But there was no alternative.

Some days before Trevor's illness, another unusual process had begun that complicated the picture further. After a private discussion it had been announced to the cast that in keeping with the collective spirit of the enterprise they were invited to take an active part in the casting process. Although, of course, we were not obliged to act on their comments, the company were invited to suggest to the directors which parts they wanted to play or indeed what parts they thought their colleagues should play. We would then use this information to guide and help the casting process. Responding privately at first to some members of the company, Trevor and John, but in particular Trevor, had begun a long, delicate process of negotiation.

In any normal RSC production, the casting begins at the top of the list with principals and works its way down. Each offer is carefully negotiated and agreed with the actor before the next stage is arrived at. There may be various financial and other

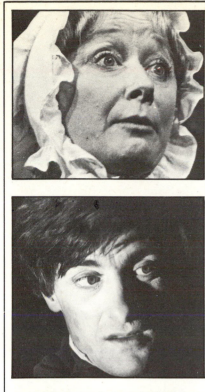

Top: Jane Downs
Centre: Roger Rees
Below: David Threlfall

artistic considerations to be discussed; for example, other parts offered in future productions. This all takes place over a long period of time and through many conversations.

With *Nicholas Nickleby* this process, complicated by the peculiar circumstances of having worked eight weeks already without casting, had just begun when Trevor Nunn was taken ill. Very few solid pieces of casting had been agreed. It was already clear by popular opinion and the directors' that Roger Rees should be Nicholas. In our own minds the directors had just about decided to cast Emily Richard as Kate. Just as this decision had been reached she told us in confidence that she would soon have to withdraw from the project for personal reasons. Although they didn't yet know it, we had also decided that Jane Downs should be Mrs Nickleby and that David Threlfall should be Smike. One or two other key parts were being negotiated, such as Ralph Nickleby, but almost no final decisions or agreements had been reached. Under normal circumstances Trevor would have continued discussions and agreements over several days until some sort of pattern emerged. If we miscalculated at all in the casting, the project would be destroyed. Already we suspected that a number of the company would leave if they were not happy with the casting. But when the fibrositis struck Trevor, the time for delay had run out.

We decided on a completely different strategy. Meeting at Trevor's flat, around his bed, we agreed that the three of us would talk together, without further negotiations with any of the actors, until we had cast the entire project. Then John and I would go in without warning and simply announce the casting to the assembled circle of actors.

For two nights we sat up together until the early hours of the morning and argued and debated the pros and cons of the casting. We tried to put together a combination of parts that would stretch each member of the company from the youngest to the most experienced. When we had finished at five o'clock on the morning of 16 February we were exhausted and worried. Many people would be deliriously happy, but a large number would be shattered. It had not been possible to please everyone. At the very beginning of the project Trevor had implied that anything was possible in the casting and that the usual hierarchy might be turned on its head. The younger and less experienced actors all hoped for a major role; we had seen the undoubted proof of that in the number of requests for particular casting that had come from Trevor's invitation for suggestions. The casting that was now on the list at five in the morning was on the whole unsurprising. The overall hierarchy had survived in most cases, although there were one or two surprises. The younger females of the company were cast in considerably larger roles than they had ever played before at the RSC, and this was also true of a few of the male parts. But with nearly a hundred per cent of the company hoping for a really major casting, there was bound to be a great deal of disappointment. When you are expecting Hamlet, even Horatio must seem momentarily as poor an offer as an attendant lord.

In our daily discussions with Andrew Snell from LWT, concerning arrangements for the next day's shooting, we mentioned that we intended to announce casting on the next day, although the company did not yet know it. Andrew pleaded for the cameras to be allowed to film the announcement. Trevor firmly refused. Andrew argued that it was these very personal and human moments behind the making of a major production that the documentary was all about. Trevor replied that it was too personal and not fair to the actors.

As John and I arrived for rehearsal the next day, Andrew asked again if he could film it, promising that only one cameraman would be present and he would stop filming at any point if requested. He argued that without such material the documentary would be an incomplete, dishonest account of *Nicholas Nickleby*. Persuaded by this, John agreed to their presence.

After a good long morning's work, we ask all the actors together into our familiar circle. Only one or two in the group know that casting is about to take place. Jane Downs was told this morning that we would like her to play Mrs Nickleby, and was thrilled to accept. But the others were shocked to hear that everything would be publicly now revealed. After the initial nervous, humorous reaction, complete silence descends upon the Conference Hall for the first time in eight weeks. Normally it is difficult in the energetic debates that rage to get a word in edgeways, or as Rod Horn put it, looking back a year later: "On the rare occasions when I had something to say it was impossible to find a moment or a second's gap in which to say it", and he had stopped politely raising his hand and learnt to barge in. Now, there is utter silence.

John explains why the casting has to be done in this unconventional way. With Trevor ill and the eight weeks trial period over there is no choice. He says that he will read out the list character by character followed by the name of the actor or actress, so that some names will be heard more than once. This way, concentration is complete until the last character has been named. Then the list will be pinned to the *Nicholas Nickleby* noticeboard, a series of boards filled with the fruits of the research. For a few days work will cease whilst the company responds to the offers to the directors (Trevor too hopes to be there by tomorrow). There are, John continues, one or two gaps in the casting that have yet to be decided. We left the gaps to give some room for manoeuvre. One character is bracketed says John and that should be self-explanatory. He means Kate Nickleby whom we wrote down as Emily Richard even though we all knew that she could not now play it. As all the other female casting revolves around the casting of Kate, we decided to leave it all as it was. Kate would now be cast outside the group. Then the reading of the list begins. The camera gently begins to whirr in the background. The characters are read out one by one.

It is much worse even than we anticipated.

As John progresses down the list, the stunned silence continues. Only a few look pleased or relieved; one or two show nothing on their faces except deep reflection. The others look at the ground. Some are red with anger and one or two try unsuccessfully to fight back tears. John and I look at each other silently, get up, pin the list on the board, and leave the room.

In that one fifteen-minute session more emotion had been released than in the whole project so far. John and I went back to report the afternoon's events to Trevor, who was still confined to bed. We really did not know what would now happen. Even in the brief moments after the reading of the list we had felt the negative response in the air. Although it was inevitable that the casting would alienate and upset some of the company whichever way it went, the reaction had been much stronger and worse than we had feared.

Work had been suspended for a week for the dust to settle whilst meetings with the actors took place. Their hostile feelings seemed to be based on principles as much as specific casting. The younger members of the company in particular felt betrayed. They had believed that the hierarchy would be turned upside down, and the casting proved that on the whole it hadn't. Although most of the actors and actresses had been given considerably larger roles or combinations of roles than ever before in their work at the RSC, they were still not happy. From first hearing that their major contribution was to be, as Alan Gill put it, "playing a character that we had to go off and look through the novel to remember who it was", they were dismayed. That was the root of much of the first wave of discontent that hit us during those first two days. Without a script

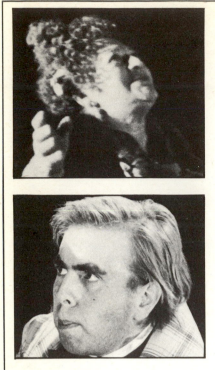

Above: Lila Kaye
Below: Tim Spall.

it was difficult for many of the company to assess what they had been given. We kept reiterating that some of the smaller roles in the novel were conceived as important contributions by David Edgar and the directors, although they seemed lost in the nine hundred pages of the original. Similarly, it was stressed how in many ways many of the less experienced members of the company had been considerably promoted in the casting, even though not to the heights that they had perhaps imagined or desired. And some of the major casting had been unusual. For example, David Threlfall, strong and healthy as he looked, was not a likely Smike, and the range of parts offered to Suzanne Bertish was extraordinary.

The company seemed to divide into four distinct groups. There were those who were content with their casting, such as Jane Downs as Mrs Nickleby, Roger Rees as Nicholas, Ben Kingsley as Squeers and Willoughby Goddard as Crummles. There was a second group who wanted further negotiation to be happy. Lila Kaye agreed to play Mrs Squeers and Mrs Crummles. Tim Spall, who played Young Wackford Squeers, was also given Folair, the Crummles Theatre Company pantomime. The third group consisted of those who were not happy at all with the announcement, but who came to feel that the offer was, after all, considerable and worth the work. They checked through the novel carefully and began to see the immense possibilities inherent in the roles they had been offered. Finally there were those who, disillusioned and angry, would not accept in any form what they had been offered. Some even turned down major roles, as they had wanted only a particular part or nothing.

After three or four days of emotionally charged discussions and negotiations, the final list was drawn up. Six people withdrew completely from the project, leaving a total of thirty-eight, from which we would lose Emily Richard by the time we arrived in Newcastle. So we had gone from the original forty-six down to thirty-seven. By the time we began again in Newcastle we would need to add five actresses to the group to complete the casting of Mrs Mantalini, Madeline Bray, Kate Nickleby and various other roles. We knew that integration of the new people would be a difficult and sensitive process after the work we had already been through together.

Morale was still very low in some places, even after the first anger and distress had subsided. There were only a few days left before the end of the season in Stratford, and we wanted to finish on a happy note before the three-week holiday and the first two-week settling-in period in Newcastle, during which time we would not rehearse *Nicholas Nickleby*.

Our now depleted group were asked to prepare for a day of Victorian festivities. We asked all the company, either individually or in groups, to organise some form of entertainment that might have been seen in Dickens's time. This could take any form and could be based on poetry, song, dance or anything else that came to mind. I provided a hastily researched collection of Victorian material as possible sources for the work, and off they went for a couple of days. The exercise might well be useful in providing ideas to be used internally within the script.

On 25 January 1980, we met for the final day's work. London Weekend Television were present again to record what Jamie Muir, their researcher, called "end of term celebrations".

And that is exactly what it seemed to be. After the tensions of casting and decision-making it was a great tonic. With the end of the Stratford season around the corner and the prospect of a three-week holiday ahead, the company were feeling in high spirits.

Edward Petherbridge, now cast as Newman Noggs, the eccentric clerk to Ralph Nickleby, limbs twitching in all directions, enacted a severely uncoordinated china plate juggler. He looked thoroughly sheepish as the plates lay in shattered fragments at his feet.

Norman Tyrrell, experienced at playing old men ever since he was a young actor, was cast as Walter Bray, the old father of the girl Nicholas falls in love with. He recited to us a very un-Victorian and very long satirical poem about the making of *Nicholas Nickleby*.

One small group of actors, including Jane Downs, cast as Mrs Nickleby, and Nick Ellsworth who was just about to leave the company, enacted a spoof of a Victorian melodrama: *The Drunkard's Dilemma*, by Andrew Sachs. As in most recent stagings of melodrama they had fun but showed beyond all doubt how not to do it! Melodrama can only work when the characters and the situation are taken seriously. The emotions of an audience can be stirred, even in ludicrous situations. After all, most television westerns or detective programmes still use the same formulae: good always triumphs over evil and the good guy gets the girl. Anyway, what they did was very funny.

John Woodvine, cast as Ralph Nickleby, and Rose Hill, cast as the miniature portrait-painter Miss La Creevy, with Hubert Rees and a few other actors performed a Victorian evening around the piano. They all sang "Just A Song at Twilight" together, and then individually sang Victorian songs or recited

Above: John Woodvine
Below: Edward Petherbridge

various texts for us. The company had become so involved with what they were doing that even this light entertainment caused tempers to rise. John Woodvine, who had never lost his temper in the theatre in the last ten years, suddenly blew up, in the Green Room, publicly, furious that all the good musicians had ended up in one group, leaving the others like himself without any musical help. A small matter perhaps in retrospect, but frustrating at the time as a certain air of competition always seemed to surface among the different groups during such exercises. But tempers cooled and Rod Horn moved helpfully between two different groups to enable the Victorian family soirée around the piano to take place.

Musically the most ambitious project to emerge was led by Roger Rees, Ben Kingsley and Roderick Horn (the group with all the good musicians!). Along with Lila Kaye, Suzanne Bertish and Julie Peasgood they performed a complete operetta. Roderick Horn set to music an episode from the novel that did not appear in the script. When Nicholas journeys to Yorkshire for the first time there are various travellers on the same coach. In the manner of *The Canterbury Tales* they tell stories to pass the time. The group chose the tale told by the merry-faced gentleman entitled *The Baron of Grogzwig*. Ben, with the help of a handlebar moustache, was the baron himself. Ben was costumed as in the story: "a fine swarthy fellow, with dark hair and large moustachios, who rode a-hunting in clothes of Lincoln green, with russet boots on his feet, and a bugle slung over his shoulder like the guard of a long stage". The baron is a happy man, surrounded by singing friends, but now, after marriage and twelve children, he is about to commit suicide. When he is visited by the "Genius of Despair and Suicide", the baron decides to see the brighter side of life and live on. Ben and his merry band imparted the story to us without the singing ever stopping, with the refrain of: "I am the Baron of Grogzwig and a very jolly baron am I", repeated throughout.

It was a very funny performance that only went to prove how difficult it would be to cut even the smallest, most peripheral incident from the final work.

In addition to recitations of poems by other members of the company, there was a final collective creation by Bob Peck, Tim Spall and Clyde Pollitt. At Clyde Pollitt's instigation they took a Victorian ballad called "The Midnight Visit", concerning a visitation by the ghost of Napoleon, and dramatised it in the manner of a Victorian penny-dreadful. They set up their booth at the far end of the Conference Hall, and in near-darkness

Ben Kingsley

brought to light the spooky story of the ghost of Napoleon:

'Twas midnight! all the lamps were dim, and dull as death the street,
It might be that the watchman slept that night upon his beat,
When lo! a heavy foot was heard to creak upon the stair,
The door revolved upon its hinge—Great Heaven!—What enters
    there?

A little man, of stately mien, with slow and solemn stride;
His hands are crossed upon his back, his coat is opened wide;
And on his vest of green he wears an eagle and a star,—
Saint George! protect us! 'tis THE MAN—the thunderbolt of war!

Is that the famous hat that waved along Marengo's ridge?
Are those the spurs of Austerlitz—the boots of Lodi's bridge?
Leads he the conscript swarm again from France's hornet hive?
What seeks the fell usurper here, in Britain, and alive?

Pale grew the Lord of Castlereagh, his tongue was parched and dry,
As in his brain he felt the glare of that tremendous eye;
What wonder if he shrunk in fear, for who could meet the glance
Of him who reared, 'mid Russian snows, the gonfalon of France?

From the side-pocket of his vest a pinch the despot took,
Yet not a whit did he relax the sternness of his look:
"Thou thoughtst the lion was afar, but he hath burst the chain—
The watchword for to-night is France—the answer St Helene . . . ."

Later in the script writing David Edgar included a recitation by the talented Miss Petowker of the Theatre Royal, Drury Lane, of another such melodramatic ballad called "The Blood-Drinker's Burial".

As the festivities ended, we felt the company morale was once again sky-high. The music, song and laughter had brought us all closer together, before the break.

With this, the first period of work on *Nicholas Nickleby* ended. Term finished and we broke up. At least, the actors went off on their holidays and Trevor, David, John and I planned the next stage of the work. Trevor was now fully recovered, and David was off to the USA in a few days to finish his work out there.

The plan was for him to come back before Newcastle rehearsals with a completed Play One—the first half of the projected two evenings of theatre. He would then work full out on Play Two whilst we rehearsed Play One, rewriting as we went along. Meanwhile, the directors would have to find by audition the actresses to fill in the gaps, and plan the next phase of the rehearsal period. In addition, the first design steps would have to be organised with John Napier. But for now, at any rate,

Nicholas Nickleby was to be left alone for a few days.

The company left Stratford, pleased to be off to exotic hot places far away from Dickensian England. I stayed in Stratford for a while to recover some sleep and reread the novel. I was glad to be leaving Stratford. Pretty though it is in the summer, it was becoming increasingly depressing in the winter. The cold, damp days were affecting all of us. The unhealthy lack of contact with other theatre companies, film or music always takes its toll by the end of the Stratford season. Like most of the company, I was looking forward to Newcastle and then the move to London. Even our work on *Nicholas Nickleby* needed an injection of fresh energy and inspiration, and London would be the natural source for it.

As I contemplated the past year with the RSC I had very mixed feelings. Before joining the company I had been a freelance director in Canada and the USA for a few years. The change to such a large company had been a shock. I had been fascinated and frustrated at watching all the cogs turn in the big machine as each production was turned out; some fine work and some poor, but all put together with intelligence and care by actors and directors alike. But few revelations had taken place— few really exciting discoveries, and few questions about the reason for all the work.

Before the beginning of *Nicholas Nickleby* I had not ever again wanted to work on another director's production. I was tired of watching a fairly predictable though supremely professional and competent process at work. The first weeks of exploratory work on *Nicholas Nickleby* had changed that feeling. I was re-energised and excited at what we were trying to do. I believed that the bored tiredness of the company had also been transformed into a new tiredness that came from having done so much to something they cared deeply about. We had changed the rules. The rehearsal period had been considerably lengthened and made structurally flexible, and the directors and the writer had already worked closely together in relative harmony. The actors had, as they always should be, been involved in artistic and practical decisions. That process had been recorded on film. From now on we would have to work against the clock in perhaps more formal rehearsal situations. I hoped that the ways we were working would not substantially change and revert to our normal rehearsal rhythms, but it was difficult yet to tell. We had come a long way in theory, but had only just begun to dig into the nine hundred pages of text: David Edgar had a lot of writing to do over the next few weeks.

We also had to integrate new members into the company into an already tightly-closed circle. Morale would be once again an all-important factor when we began again in Newcastle, and I knew that, as ever, Trevor Nunn would ultimately be responsible for that.

As I walked along the banks of the Avon in the actor-deserted Stratford I felt that some of the roots of our work in the theatre had been dug up and examined. Why do we bother with it all anyway? What is there that needs to be told and what is the best way to tell it? What is the way to create rich characters that are larger than life but drawn directly from it? How do you contact an audience and share your story with them? As Trevor once said to me: "When people come into the theatre we must try to change their lives". I threw some stale bread to the ducks and walked back to the ugly building of the Stratford Memorial Theatre to pack up my already large pile of script, extracts and notes and a copy of *Nicholas Nickleby* to reread before Newcastle. Even the swans had gone.

John McEnery

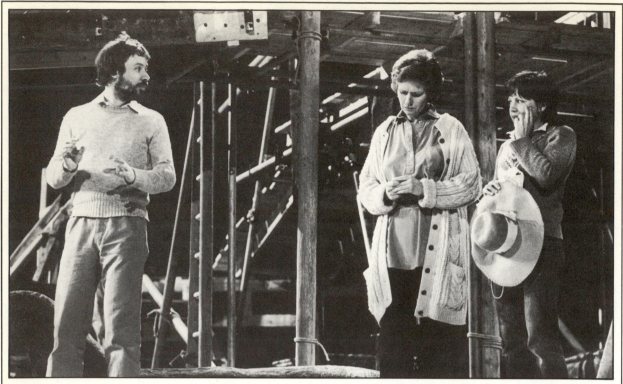

THE MOVE NORTH

John Caird rehearsing Madame Mantalini and Miss Knag

Many suntans later the Newcastle season began. The first two weeks before *Nicholas Nickleby* rehearsals started again felt very much like a school trip abroad. It is a wonderful feeling for the Royal Shakespeare Company to be in Newcastle. There is a genuine excitement in the town when they arrive like a rock band on tour, moving into small hotels and family houses. The company is welcomed with warmth. Instead of performing for the large numbers of tourists who make the pilgrimage to Stratford, the RSC has come to its audience. The people there know how difficult it is for the company to tour and appreciate the fact that Newcastle has become its North England home for six weeks every year. The tickets usually sell out in advance of our arrival and the queues form every day for return tickets. The actors go out into schools and colleges, organised by Maurice Daniels, Head of Special Projects at the RSC, to meet their audiences and demonstrate their work. They are given complimentary tickets to the local cinemas and sports clubs, and are invited to numerous parties and official receptions.

Everyone is pleased to have time to shop! In Stratford the company rehearses every day and performs every night, and the shops close at five o'clock. In Newcastle there is the luxury of films and clubs. It is like releasing a crowd of prisoners at a party.

The Theatre Royal is an excellent theatre to perform in.

Although a large auditorium, it feels intimate to the actors, in comparison to the barn-like emptiness of the Stratford Memorial Theatre. The actors feel much more contact with their audience, who in turn respond enthusiastically to them. Although there are local reviews, the pressures of the Stratford and London press nights, when life or death is decreed on the basis of one relatively immature performance, are absent. The company know their work well by this time and have confidence in it. In Newcastle the performance can be refined and problems solved before going to London.

Normally, apart from brief preparations at each opening, there is no rehearsal in Newcastle. This time the celebrations and relaxations were intruded upon by the continuance of the *Nicholas Nickleby* saga. After two weeks of establishing themselves in Newcastle, the actors sat in their familiar circle, and it was extended again as the company were introduced to their new colleagues.

Kate Nickleby, the role most wanted by the actresses already in the company, was to be played by Susan Littler—not an obvious choice for the role, perhaps. She was dark and not as delicate as Emily Richard, the original choice, but with a wonderful sense of humour and irony: a good match for Roger Rees, but not at all what Dickens might have imagined. Susan is a very experienced actress with a particular quality of strength and determination, that would we hoped help to solve the problem of the ineffective heroine conceived by Dickens.

Juliet Hammond-Hill was cast as Madeline Bray, Nicholas Nickleby's future wife. Juliet is photogenically attractive, with carefully frizzed blonde hair and natural elegance. Most of her background was in television work rather than the stage, and John Caird had been particularly intrigued with her performance as a French resistance worker in *Secret Army*. He and Trevor had done two workouts with her earlier when they were casting *The Merry Wives of Windsor*.

Thelma Whiteley joined us to play Mrs Mantalini, married to the extravagant, wasteful Mr Mantalini played by John McEnery. Thelma is an actress with many leading credits on the stage. Her thorough rehearsal approach and instinct for humour were just what was needed to fill that gap. Trevor had first worked with her in Coventry in 1962, and had been waiting for the right opportunity to involve her with the RSC.

Two other actresses completed the new female contingent: Clare Travers-Deacon and Sharon Bower. Clare, short with big eyes hiding behind large glasses that covered most of her face,

John Caird not directing traffic but rehearsing Kate Nickleby (Susan Littler) as a milliner, and Juliet Hammond-Hill

was often cast as a little girl, even though she was twenty-seven years old. Clare was a marvellous character actress to add to the company, and with her infectious laugh and easy manner was the first to blend into the group. When Roger Rees heard that Clare Travers-Deacon and Juliet Hammond-Hill were joining us he solemnly declared, "Well, that's four already, who are the others?".

Sharon Bower, a tall woman with long brownish red hair and a strong physique, could not have been more different from Clare. Shy by nature, she took time to feel at home in the company, but her beautiful and powerful singing voice soon came into its own in the early days of rehearsal in Newcastle.

Finally, there was one male newcomer to the group, Andrew Hawkins. He joined the company to take over a vacant part in the *Julius Caesar* production and was also invited to join *Nicholas Nickleby*. Tall, aristocratic in manner, and full of enthusiasm for the project, Andrew was an additional strength, and was soon fated to have to understudy Roger Rees as Nicholas.

Casting was now complete and rehearsals had to commence at full speed. Trevor went back to work on the Squeers family at Dotheboys Hall, with Ben Kingsley as Squeers; he had originally presented him in the scene directed by David Edgar as a cold, menacing figure. Lila Kaye was now Mrs Squeers, Suzanne Bertish Fanny Squeers, and Tim Spall young Wackford, the schoolmaster's son. Tim is one of the most unusual actors in the RSC. He trained at the Royal Academy of Dramatic Arts and joined the company a year before *Nicholas Nickleby* began rehearsing. Accustomed from years of practice to transforming his normal East End accent into perfect BBC English, Tim is an actor full of surprises. He has an acute ability to observe and understand the characters he portrays, and his naturally anarchic approach to his work is always exciting to watch. Tim hardly ever spoke in the hours of discussions, but when he did it always came straight from the heart. One day he will make a strange and extraordinary Hamlet.

Working with this Squeers family, and with Cathryn Harrison as Phib the servant and David Threlfall as Smike, Trevor now began to create a home environment behind the nightmare cruelty of Dotheboys Hall. Why shouldn't the Squeerses be a loving family? Even the guards in World War II concentration camps must have had families and loved ones at home. Ben worked away at the most difficult task of humanising Mr Squeers. Did he really believe in some perverse way that his horrific treatment of the boys was a moral necessity? Does

Ben Kingsley reads a new piece of script at the Rainbow Theatre

Squeers have a necessary function in running that kind of Yorkshire school for the boys discarded by the rest of society? Who else would keep them alive? Ben clasped at these questions as he began to build up the character behind the evil Phiz mask.

Meanwhile John Caird, aided by me, explored the life of the pupils themselves. Each boy now formally cast was asked to create a background for himself. Some had names mentioned in the novel, others invented them themselves. They were then asked to imagine as full as possible a past to the boy: place of upbringing, age, parental treatment, illnesses, feelings about the school, and so on. In particular they were asked to find out why they were there. Through disfigurement or other social cause or pressure such as illegitimacy or remarried parents.

To help this process, an interrogation of each boy took place. We formed a semi-circle of chairs and placed one boy in front of us at a time. Anyone there could ask him or her questions. What is your name? How old are you? How long have you been in the school? What do you dream at night? Do you remember your parents? Etc., etc.

Having created their personal case histories, they were then asked to interact in character and establish a social environment at the school. What was the internal hierarchy? What was the pecking order? Who was friends with whom? What about Young Wackford? Did the boys fear him? Did they hate him? Did they simply hold him in contempt?

An immense variety of characters of different ages and case-histories emerged. Juliet Hammond-Hill sounded shell-shocked as Sprouter whose "father killed my mother". The surly, aggressive Jackson, played by Nicholas Gecks, also doubling as the innocent young Lord Verisopht; tall, thin, resentful, with the manner of a bully. Teddy Kempner, short, sharp-featured, curly hair, was the blind Peters. The older Snawley, full of resistance to his new environment, was played by the versatile Lucy Dale. The crippled Cobbey was played by John Matshikiza, the only black actor in the company; frustrated by playing Shakespearean servants and token blacks he hoped that *Nicholas Nickleby* would allow him a chance to prove that directors needn't be paranoid about black actors playing in an English classical repertory. (One day a black actor will be able to play Hamlet without everybody thinking that the production is necessarily about racial harmony in Elizabethan England.) Ian East, incredibly thin, over thirty but looking like one of Dickens's "boys with the faces of old men", played Roberts, hands always twitching and moving nervously. Stephen Rashbrook, at twenty the youngest man in the company, played the docile Belling, instantly nicknamed "Baby Belling" by the actors, who always had his hand interlocked with that of Juliet Hammond-Hill, Sprouter. Christopher Ravenscroft, tall and strong in build, transformed himself into Mobbs, the boy who walks with uncoordinated movements and permanently disfigured knees. Neil Philips played the bully McTaggart. Alan Gill played the submissive and quiet Graymarsh. Mark Tandy was the slow-thinking, slow-moving Bolder. Bill Maxwell, short and round-faced, played the ever-eager-to-please Tompkins. Terence Harvey played the boy with the disfigured nose and nasal voice, Jennings. Andrew Hawkins played Coates and Clare Travers-Deacon played the terrified younger Snawley. Sharon Bower completed the cast as Pitcher, whose mind is very slow.

This class of 1836 of Dotheboys Hall worked together over a period of days to define and fix their characters and relationships. At first their case histories were over-intellectual; later the physical deformities emerged more markedly. In the midst of them were the malicious young Wackford Squeers and the pathetic Smike. Tim Spall developed Wackford as he pushed and hit the smaller boys and Smike mercilessly, and smiled as the older ones were beaten by his father Mr Squeers.

Meanwhile, David Threlfall slowly immersed himself in the character of Smike, giving himself up completely to the role. David seems to have to become the character he is playing in every emotional and physical detail before it feels right. From the earlier collective research projects, from evidence in the novel about diet, and from what he himself had learnt about common diseases of the period such as rickets, he could envisage how Smike should move. He discovered that a protein-deficient diet causes a deficiency of calcium in the bones, so that Smike's body would be weak all over. Later he added problems with the respiratory system and the collapsed lung and consumptive symptoms that led to his death. As time went on the medical aspects retreated a little, allowing the emotional side to dominate his portrayal as he began to enter the psyche and emotions of Smike and discover his attitudes to the people and things around him. The difficulty was that neither David nor the directors had yet grasped the fact that Smike was latently intelligent.

Before the Dotheboys work had begun there was one other new direction in our work. During the break we had met with Stephen Oliver, the composer, who had already produced a mass of inventive musical ideas. He had rapidly written scores for various passages in the novel and an operetta for possible performance by the Crummles Theatre Company. Trevor and John had asked him to concentrate on one particular passage that represented a point in the play that needed a release that only music could provide. Although Trevor, John and I had grave misgivings on the subject of operatic rendition of text, we needed to give it a try.

Stephen's arrival in Newcastle happened to coincide with that of London Weekend Television. Already in Stratford we had felt the effects of their presence. Concentration had been low, particularly from the directors. Much poor rehearsal had taken place and time had been lost. None of us wanted to be filmed at work, so we decided, generously, to hand over the day's work to Stephen. As he arrived off the train we planned for him to take the session. When he arrived at rehearsal we informed him that the day was all his and he could try his experiments on the chosen passage. "By the way," said Trevor, "I believe the television cameras will be there."

He claimed later to have been terrified, but turned out to be a total celluloid triumph. Peering through his thick-lensed glasses, over-articulating every final syllable of each sentence, his hands energetically blocking out imaginary notes in the air and chattering wittily non-stop, he won over both actors and cameras.

Stephen poured out energy as he moulded the company into a singing ensemble. He divided up the different ranges of voices and orchestrated the passage with them into a series of different rhythms, within the score he had prepared in advance.

The passage was yet again one concerning a journey. As in many of the previous exercises we wanted to communicate the experience of travelling. The picaresque nature of the novel was still the touchstone at the centre. This particular example showed the transition from Smike's miserable and unhappy memories of fear as a child to a mood of unfettered joy and exhilaration as he and Nicholas journey away from the city into the open country.

It was by this time within an hour of noon, and although a dense vapour still enveloped the city they had left as if the very breath of its busy people hung over their schemes of gain and profit and found greater attraction there than in the quiet region above, in the open country it was clear and fair. Occasionally in some low spots they came upon patches of mist which the sun had not yet driven from their strongholds; but these were soon passed, and as they laboured up the hills beyond, it was pleasant to look down and see how the sluggish mass rolled heavily off before the cheering influence of day. A broad fine honest sun lighted up the green pastures and dimpled water with the semblance of summer, while it left the travellers all

Nicholas and Smike having fun on the road to Portsmouth

the invigorating freshness of that early time of year. The ground seemed elastic under their feet; the sheep-bells were music to their ears; and exhilarated by exercise, and stimulated by hope, they pushed onwards with the strength of lions.

The day wore on, and all these bright colours subsided, and assumed a quieter tint, like young hopes softened down by time, or youthful features by degrees resolving into the calm and serenity of age.

Stephen Oliver believed that a musical transition from greyness to ecstasy, created with the voices of the entire company, would best reflect this process of change. Although it was brilliantly conceived and successfully organised, and completely different from any of the previous solutions, we agreed that such a technique would have to be used cautiously and rarely. Stephen would, I am sure, have been happy to score the entire production if given half the chance.

The exercise was another good example to us of the need not to restrict ourselves by the fetters of a particular style. As many different techniques and ideas as possible would have to be created and utilised to do justice to the immense variety of Dickens's creation.

David Edgar, as usual tuning in sympathetically to what other minds were thinking, worked through the passage, changing words and phrases and tidying up the metre with Stephen. Later, Trevor Nunn added a physical enactment of the journey by Nicholas and Smike that worked concurrently with the sung narrative.

Other new areas of the novel were opened up in these weeks in Newcastle, not all of which I will relate in detail here. The political satire already implicit from the muffin scene onwards was explored again in one specific scene. When Nicholas, unemployed, is looking desperately for a job, he applies to be secretary to Mr Gregsbury, Honourable Member of Parliament. We changed his name to Sir Matthew Pupker to be consistent: we wanted in this scene the same Member of Parliament who was present in the muffin scene. Sir Matthew, played by David Lloyd Meredith, is engaged with a group of complaining constituency members who are appalled at his record since they voted him in as their representative. Nicholas listens as Sir Matthew refuses to discuss their criticism or agree to resign and shows them the door. During the research we had discovered that one of the political topics of the 1830s was the threat of a Russian invasion of Afghanistan. The Russian tanks rolled in there whilst we were rehearsing in Stratford. David Edgar added a few references to that when allowing full vent to Sir Matthew's expansive declaration of patriotism. During the first weeks of performance the reference amused the audience. By the second run, alas, headlines had changed.

After the delegates leave Nicholas is interviewed and is outraged by the list of duties that Sir Matthew suggests he must do.

Sir Matthew Pupker receives the complaints of his constituents

In fact the duties cover all the work supposed to be done by Sir Matthew himself.

Even with a great deal of rehearsal the scene just never seemed to work. In theory, the satire seemed good, the subject appropriate: but in practice it was tedious. Trevor, John and I directed it over the next weeks from time to time and David tried various rewrites. After much cutting and trial and error and speeding up of the performance it came closer to being effective. Only in the final days before opening the show did it come together with a major last-minute rewrite, which was handed to David Lloyd Meredith just before the dress rehearsal. However, all the attempts to find a final devastating, witty retort from Nicholas

Nicholas plays "Speculation" with Fanny Squeers, John Browdie and Tilda Price. Phib looks on

were doomed to fail. We were probably wrong even to try. Trevor felt that there was, perhaps inevitably, a quality of revue sketch about the scene, and I, and I think he, wondered if that quality really fitted in with the rest of the play.

Another scene that received direction from all three of us before the opening in London was the tea-party scene at Dotheboys Hall. Fanny Squeers, played by Suzanne Bertish, considering herself in love with Nicholas, invites him to tea. Also present is her best friend Tilda Price, played by Julie Peasgood, and her fiancé John Browdie, played by Bob Peck. The reluctant Nicholas and the others drink tea, play at cards, and end up in an argument as Nicholas flirts with Tilda Price. As our first example of situation comedy, the scene was immediately joyous to rehearse. The social humour of the grotesquely over-dressed girls and the clumsy John Browdie always saying and doing the wrong thing, was an important clue to the nature of Dickens's satire. Dickens in this scene plays for the class aspirations of the miller's daughter and the schoolmaster's daughter and compares it to the rough but honest John Browdie. Being a Victorian gentleman or lady is more for Dickens than affecting genteel manners and wearing fine clothes. Nicholas reveals a certain snobbery and disdain as he indulges in the pleasures of tea with the attractive Miss Price at the expense of the feelings of Miss Squeers. Roger eagerly clutched at the chance to begin building the imperfect Nicholas, rather than the faultless hero.

Another piece of new territory opened up in Newcastle was the first scene with the Kenwigs family. This was the best example to date of a small subplot that could easily be cut or reduced to a shadow in any normal adaptation, but for Trevor this family represented the touchstone of our style. Through them we could achieve a perspective on the other characters in the play. Dickens satirises their ordinariness. Trevor believed that they were the starting point from which a standard of Victorian ordinariness could be derived for the actors, before moving on too fast towards the more extraordinary social environments and characters in the novel. He was sure that the detail of our work must lead towards a comedy of "recognition". If we could find a style which could embrace documentary reality, and Jonsonian observation, we could then grow outwards from that point. He was also attracted to the Kenwigses as brilliant comic creations.

The Kenwigses and all their guests are gathered in an enormous church hall in Newcastle. Trevor herds them all into a tiny enclosure in one corner of the room. Before they arrived, Trevor and I marked off with chairs a tiny area of a few square feet in an oblong shape. Within are packed tightly together various odd chairs and stools. The actors all forced their way in, crammed against each other hardly able to negotiate their way across the space without elbowing and upsetting furniture. "That's it," says Trevor, "that's the room for the party!" In that one of the Kenwigses' two rooms the party was to take place. Trevor remembers images of childhood in small rooms, always over-filled with bulky furniture so that the door can barely open.

Trevor insists on a gentle unprojected performance, just a quiet, domestic at-home scene. It is actually very difficult for some of the company to speak and act naturalistically. There is

Above: Morleena Kenwigs (Clare Travers-Deacon) performs her figure dance for her parents' guests

Below: Miss Petowker recites "The Blood Drinker's Burial" at the Kenwigs' party

always an instinct to exaggerate a character that is known to be funny. After a while it begins to work and Trevor begins his usual microscopically detailed examination of each thought, word and deed. The Kenwigses, packed into a claustrophobic corner of a Newcastle church hall, are born.

When the Kenwigs scenes were eventually transferred onto the stage, the geography and dimensions of the room stayed exactly the same. In the middle of the expanse of the Aldwych stage the Kenwigses' home was created on a small platform covered with tightly packed chairs and tables, like a tiny life-boat packed full of survivors, the scene stayed just the way it was in rehearsal in the middle of the stage. Similarly, the danger of overperformance would also always remain.

KG1 was the inscription at the top of the first page of that scene, translated as Kenwigs 1. This was David Edgar's code for the scene. Instead of numbering the pages and scenes, he invented his own system of scene identification. Knowing that the scenes would in all probability be swapped round many times before the final order was agreed on, he was taking no chances. He decided to allocate a code for each plot, followed by the number of the scene within it. Thus we had already rehearsed DH1 and DH2 (Dotheboys Hall, first and second scenes). This seemed simplicity itself until the rewrites began. David's second attempt at DH1 became DH1 R1 (Dotheboys Hall 1, rewrite 1). That was just about okay until scenes sometimes became merged together. By the time David produced CH3/AG1 R1, the company had given up trying to follow the system. One day when I looked up at a cross on the wall of the rehearsal room, and saw INRI inscribed below, I thought for a moment that David's system had gone a little too far.

In spite of the mirth that David's system produced, the writer had been a jump ahead of the directors. By the time we were halfway through Newcastle rehearsals the structure was becoming a major problem. Before the end of Newcastle we had to have Play One fully organised. Only parts of Play Two had as yet been written.

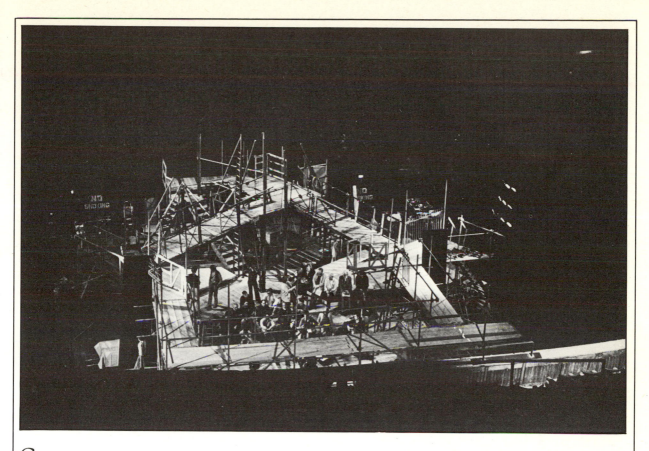

STRUCTURE AND DESIGN

The first discussions about structure had begun back in Stratford, although even by the end of the Stratford rehearsal period few scenes had actually been written or rehearsed. The early decision to commit ourselves to two plays still seemed feasible by the middle of Newcastle. We now knew most of the material that the first play would consist of, but Play Two was still largely an unknown quantity.

The structural problems came right to the centre of the question: what is the difference between a novel and a play? Although many of the answers seem obvious, in reality they are more subtle. Most schools and universities still insist on approaching plays as though they are novels. Play texts are analysed and discussed as though the written form is the end of the artistic process and that no performance ever exists. The final part of any dramatic process, a performance with an audience, is as important as the words on the page. The performance of a work changes the entire nature of that artistic creation. With an audience and a company of actors, a living process is under way that is intrinsically different from a final prose work, designed only to be read.

The set at the Rainbow Theatre

Dickens wrote *Nicholas Nickleby* in instalments to be read by the public over a considerable period of time. The work is full of moments of suspense that hover as cliffhangers at the end of an instalment, sustaining suspense until the next issue. As in a television serial, the dramatic rhythm of the instalments peak in the centre and again at the end. In this way, different areas of the novel become almost self-sufficient—enjoyable as entities in themselves. Each section has its own focus and overall structure. For a dramatic adaptation, the problems are very different.

An audience has its own particular ability to respond to the work at a given moment in time. They cannot put down the work or finish one section and continue the next days later. The internal structure and rhythms of the dramatic work must recognise this. The epic nature of Dickens's novel has a relatively free time context in which to work. Days and weeks and months can go by in a few pages or over a few hundred pages of a novel. Characters can be described in Yorkshire one moment, whilst someone else is simultaneously depicted at work in London or Portsmouth. Part of a novelist's skill is the ability to juggle with different balls, keeping two or three plots, or in Dickens's case many more, moving in harmony with each other. On the stage, this freedom is inhibited. Dickens can introduce characters with lengthy descriptions, but on stage there is only a little time for the audience to become familiar with each character, to understand and feel what their world is about. Similarly, mood and atmosphere take time to create for a live audience. The bleakness of Dotheboys Hall and the personalities of Smike, Squeers, Mrs Squeers and Fanny take time to engage an audience fully.

In the novel, Dickens is able to jump backwards and forwards between the primary and secondary plot concerning Kate Nickleby, but on stage the physical realities of a set and furniture limit the amount of continual geographic transposition. However stripped down and simplified a setting is, it still has to be established and then taken away, and too much changing can become tedious. In a novel there is no such problem: events can meander through several locations, one after another, in what seems to be a matter of weeks or months. On stage the time structure and geography need to be telescoped and focused.

Bearing this in mind, we had concluded in Stratford that the first play should consist of certain incidents and characters only. If the work was to take place over two evenings, each part had to be complete in itself and simultaneously part of the whole story. An audience should be able to enjoy as a complete theatrical experience any one evening in the theatre, but should be

The Nickleby family meet Ralph

encouraged to see the complete story. This would immediately present a dramatic structural problem quite different from anything that Dickens had to contend with. In essence, we would have to create a structure for the first half of the play that, like Dickens's episodes, was internally complete and yet looked ahead to another day.

We decided that Play One was to deal with the first meeting of Mrs Nickleby, Nicholas and Kate with Ralph Nickleby, with Nicholas's time as a teacher at Dotheboys Hall and his consequent escape with Smike. Alongside that plot would be the story of Kate's employment with the Mantalinis. Then we would go on to Nicholas's fortunes with the Crummles Theatre Company and Kate's troubles with Sir Mulberry Hawk. The play would end in some way with an upward movement of celebration with Nicholas in his final moments with the Crummles Theatre Company. Also included along the way would be the extra plots such as the Kenwigses and the visit of Nicholas to Sir Matthew Pupker.

The first area that had been debated at length was the introduction of Sir Mulberry Hawk. Originally it had been argued that all the Sir Mulberry Hawk plot should be dealt with in the second play, but after discussion it was agreed that the threat to Kate is not serious or interesting enough if her only problems are with the Mantalinis. With Nicholas suffering at Dotheboys Hall, Kate's parallel journey needs to be also intense and hazardous. It was therefore agreed that Sir Mulberry's first attempt on Kate's honour must happen somehow in Play One.

The other part that took a long time to evolve was the ending. Trevor had said very early on that the first play should end with a Crummles Theatre Company performance—everything we had always dreaded seeing from that company. He also thought that it should perhaps be Shakespeare. Dickens refers to their Shakespearean performances in the novel and David Edgar, acting on these references, proposed *Romeo and Juliet*, adding, in the nineteenth-century tradition, his own happy ending. As in Tate's *Lear* when Cordelia marries Edgar, David offered us a living Romeo and Juliet happily married, and families reconciled and united.

This process of sharing an idea was perfectly shown in this ending of Play One. Trevor proposed a general idea, David offered a specific example. Then it suddenly struck Trevor that the choice of *Romeo and Juliet* was even more appropriate than any of us had realised. The plot of *Romeo and Juliet*, in particular the scenes concerning Capulet and Juliet, was a strong parallel to Kate's journey in the novel. Trevor went on to suggest that the climax and end to our play could be rapidly built up by crossing backwards and forwards from the one plot to the other, indicating the parallels and increasing the suspense. David used as a link between the two plots an idea suggested right back in the early improvisations when one actor, choosing the character of Smike for his solo performance, acted out Smike trying unsuccessfully to learn the apothecary's speech from *Romeo and Juliet*. The final scene that David ingeniously moulded together harnessed all these different thoughts and elements. In rehearsal, a few weeks before the opening in London, the problem of realising in practical terms what he had written came to a head. But again by a co-operative system of three directors and two designers working together we ended up with a method of production that allowed the two plots to cross-fade into each other without stopping as their momentum builds towards the climax. A single chaise-longue is used as a piece of furniture in the *Romeo and Juliet* performance and in the scene between Sir Mulberry and Kate, thus uniting the two physically as well as thematically. John Caird cleverly turned the theory into practice as he worked on the scene.

The other key problem was the specific scene order and the choice of interval. We agreed that we must have a single interval that would in some way divide the two basic halves of the play between Dotheboys Hall and the Crummles Theatre Company. The precise moment was varied in rehearsal and finally chosen at the point of Nicholas discovering Smike and agreeing to take him along on his travels. In this way the emotional line of story concerning Smike was linked with the plot centre, Nicholas, at the end of the first dramatic sweep of the adaptation. The order of scenes was also variable; David Edgar's coding system allowed any combination or order. The main decision was to present Dotheboys Hall as a fairly solid block of scenes to establish it physically, emotionally and atmospherically for the audience before switching back to the Kate plot at the Mantalinis. The other scenes were juggled around many times for structural and physical reasons of scene changing and continuity.

By far the bigger problem was to structure Play Two. By the end of Newcastle David had written about a third of the second play and we already realised how long it would have to be to include all the necessary plots and new characters. We left the serious structural questions to be decided in London. At this point we had enough to worry about with the first play, which we feared might be twice as long as it should be. We still could not estimate its length at all accurately and suspected that he had about seven hours' worth of material. David was still struggling to get further ahead with Play Two, but was held back by the constant need to rewrite scenes from Play One. He made the fatal tactical error of staying at the Swallow Hotel in Newcastle where Trevor and John were staying. Wisely, I stayed on the other side of town, although I ended up most of each night talking at the Swallow too. David was constantly in meetings until the early hours of the morning or had visits and questions from people dropping in on him. When alone writing, he had the constant fear of the three of us a few doors along the corridor cutting and rewriting his text. He found it even worse when he knew we were having a meeting he was not invited to. The late nights disturbed his rhythm of writing in the mornings, and he found himself more and more behind with his schedule. The emotional strain of simultaneous rewrites and new scenes in another play was enough to stop anyone in their tracks.

The other pressing problem was the design. We had rehearsed most of one of the two plays, but without any definite

Detail from the set

sense of physical context. So far we had simply used any bits of furniture and odd handprops that were available; there was no real sense of continuity or physical production. But only now was John Napier free from his work on the epic production of John Barton's *The Greeks*. He had already formed his own design team, with Dermot Hayes as co-designer and John Thompson as assistant, and he now came to Newcastle for a crucial meeting with Trevor, John Caird and me.

Back in Stratford at the end of the season, Trevor talked about the design in an interview for London Weekend: "We're going to be asking John Napier to provide us with a space that all of the actors can surround if they wish to, that will have some sort of constructivist look about it. It will be a machine that will help us to present the play, but I suspect that it won't be pictorial; I mean it won't be a view of London in the 1830s. Obviously, its textures and the shapes that it employs, materials that it employs, must be evocative. I think that the design must have a very dynamic relationship with the audience, and I think that it's quite possible that we must be able to get into the audience and back from the audience into the playing area very easily, perhaps at more than one level of the auditorium. We must be able to do that. My hunch is that the textures will be quite rough, but it's unlikely to be colourful. I think there's so much richness in that story, so much richness in the characters and the wealth or the glamour when it does appear in the novel, it's so specialised that I think the prevailing image must not be colourful or exuberant, I mean I think the exuberance has got to come from the performance."

Weeks later in Newcastle, Trevor reiterated these feelings. He talked about Russian constructivist sets, rough textures, audience contact, sawdust, wood and nineteenth-century industrial structures, but did not define exactly what he meant. He wanted a non-pictorial, truthful reflection of the period, unsentimental and harsh. John Caird and I agreed with what he was saying, but David was unhappy—he still held on to long-cherished dreams of flying scenery, or mechanical devices. Another of Trevor's ideas was that everything should be open and exposed to the audience, with set changes simply achieved by the actors themselves, and even costume changes on stage. David was horrified at the thought of costume racks on the stage, which sounded like fringe theatre of the sixties.

Wondering how radical Trevor really intended to be when he talked about rough sets and true reflections of society, I ironically proposed to him the idea of open sewers running through

John Napier

the Aldwych auditorium to reflect street conditions in the 1830s. But Trevor would not rise to the bait. John Napier, probably feeling suspicious of Trevor's declarations in the way that I had, also mischievously challenged him. Did Trevor really want such a crude and simple design? John knew him well enough to suspect otherwise. Trevor reaffirmed his beliefs, but John still did not believe that Trevor wanted something that would not actually look beautiful. He left for London the next day, confused and troubled.

The costumes were less of a problem. We all agreed that in the short time available it would not be possible to make them all. Therefore, John Napier and Dermot Hayes would select clothes to rent from big costumiers in London that had vast stocks of Victorian clothes. John Napier would then painstakingly create a costume from pieces of different clothing for each character, bearing in mind that all actors played multiple parts and few complete changes would be possible. Some costumes when really necessary would have to be designed and made. As few wigs and beards as possible would be used. Each actor would have a basic simple Victorian dress costume which would be added to and changed as the two plays moved forward. The costume selection process was to be done in London some weeks later.

About ten days later after two trips to London Trevor came back excited with what the designers had come up with. Trevor sketched for me what John Napier had shown him, and I began to share his enthusiasm. The basic design was a large wooden stage that joined completely with the auditorium. Surrounding the stage on two levels was a large scaffolding structure. Like a bridge it spanned the proscenium width of the upstage area and was built out right around the dress circle of the house. Another runway of wood was built right out from the stage through the middle of the stalls seats. The scaffolding structure had ladders and steps connecting it at multiple points to the main stage area and was decorated with various pieces of scrap metal and rusted pieces of Victorian-looking ironwork. The towers of metal looked like Victorian bridges or skyline connections between roofs of London houses of the period. Into the big open wooden central stage area could be rolled two wooden trucks on wheels. Each truck was an acting area in itself, one large and one relatively small. The large truck, which could be divided into two sections, moved across from upstage left to centre stage and the smaller and lower truck moved from upstage right to downstage centre. Both could be visible at all times even when being fitted with furniture for a particular scene. Any furniture or props or costumes could be stored in one of the many areas around the stage within the scaffolding structure, and visible to the audience. It really would be a non-mechanical set of large proportions—if it could ever be actually built. At this stage, we did not know the costs and practical problems involved; that would be a later crisis to deal with.

When I saw this remarkable design I could hardly believe that it was the result of our meeting in Newcastle. With so many voices offering so many different opinions I could not conceive how John Napier could have understood enough about what was going on to have produced what I now saw drawn before me. A year later I asked Trevor what actually happened when he went down to London, and Trevor admitted that he had had a long conversation with John Napier. Not for the last time in the project, he decided that he had to act alone for a while. Realising that John was confused, he gave him certain touchstones to work from. First of all he reminded him of the original permanent set he had designed for the 1976 Stratford season. It was an extraordinarily anarchic, off-centre design that was very ungeometrical and rough. For practical reasons it had not been used, but Trevor had been impressed by it and it had stuck firmly in his head. He also reminded John of a walk they had had together through Covent Garden a long time ago. As they had walked through the various building works, Trevor had pointed out the scaffolding everywhere and remarked to John how much it felt like the teeming nineteenth-century metropolis of industrial England. Finally he went through lots of books of photographs with John Napier and found four or five key reference points. One in particular was of a nineteenth-century waggon, a railway truck which inspired John with the idea of moving platforms with wheels that could be seen. By the end of the meeting, John had had images in his head, concrete images unlike the impressionistic fragments that had emerged in Newcastle.

Overnight John Napier changed the direction of our work. He fired us with an immense excitement and gave us a focus for all we were doing. We had desperately lacked a concrete physical context. Since the early experimental work and the beginning of the more formal rehearsal process of scenes, we had been working in many ways in a vacuum. Individual characters in scenes were growing well, but a sense of the whole was lacking. Trevor in particular was unhappy at working in rehearsal without a specific sense of geography in the space. Now, it was possible to go into rehearsal and define the physical production. Scenes

could be begun and ended; until now the focus was on the middle, due to the insecurity we had all felt about how one scene should end and the next begin. The suggested design now made it possible to devise a scene change and a continuity with which to bind it all together. At last I felt that the RSC were working the right way round. The design should never really come before rehearsal. It is so much more liberating to have a design that suits what has been discovered and explored in a rehearsal situation. Suddenly the design concept became a liberating influence rather than a straitjacket.

We left the explanation of the set to the actors for London, when a model would be available for the company to see. But

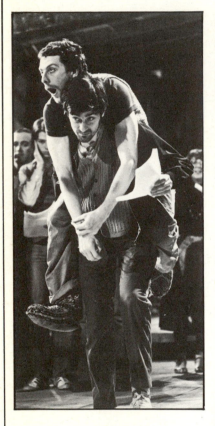

Above: Nicholas and Smike rehearse at the Rainbow Theatre

Centre and below: Nicholas and Smike

even now they sensed the new positive thinking that it seemed to have encouraged in the directors.

Another happy and revelatory process in Newcastle was our visit to a disused Victorian theatre. Lovingly restored and now serving as a cinema, it represents a beautiful example of mid-nineteenth-century stage-machinery. The building itself is partly original and partly rebuilt. Although belonging to a slightly later date, the facilities would have been almost identical to those in the theatres where the Crummles Theatre Company might have performed. We arranged for the company to visit here to help understand the atmosphere and background for the Crummles Theatre Company and their visit to Portsmouth. It achieved exactly that. We spent some hours wandering about imagining ourselves back in Dickens's England. We had an in-formed guided tour of the backstage and below-stage areas. The latter was an extraordinary revelation to most of us. The soph-isticated, complex understage machinery of various trapdoors and grooves fascinated all of us and helped to bring to life the written accounts of nineteenth-century theatre techniques, and the references in *Nicholas Nickleby*. From that day on the Crummles Theatre Company had a sense of the theatre in Ports-mouth as a temporary home on the road.

We were accompanied by the television crew on our visit. Trevor had intended to rehearse a Crummles scene there, but the visit backstage and around the auditorium had exhausted nearly all our time. With only twenty minutes to go Trevor felt that he had disappointed London Weekend Television, so de-cided to put on a performance for the cameras with a last-minute rehearsal. He was embarrassed to discover that none of the act-ing company had a clue what was going on as he rushed about pretending to rehearse. Andrew Snell promised not to use the soundtrack and Trevor had to explain later to the bewildered actors that there was a logical explanation for it all.

One final visit that took place during our time in Newcastle must be mentioned. Roger Rees and David Threlfall took advan-tage of a day off to drive over to Greta Bridge in Yorkshire to explore the setting of Dotheboys Hall. Although they had worked together for a year at Stratford they were not particu-larly close. They both came from very different backgrounds, social and theatrical. David Threlfall, a very young and uncon-ventional actor from a fringe theatre background, contrasted markedly with Roger Rees, a little older and more experienced and of a mainly conventional RSC background. Since deciding that art school was not the place for him, he had taken up acting.

Separately, both had begun to build their characters, but the closeness and intimate stage relationship that was needed did not yet exist between them. The journey to Greta Bridge suddenly changed that. They looked around at the supposed site of Dotheboys Hall, and the more bleak patch of land that a local suggested was the real site of Mr Shaw's Academy for Boys. They found the gravestone of a small boy of London parents who had died there: his name was Digby—the pseudonym given to Smike by Nicholas at Portsmouth. They were both deeply moved by that lonely grave. As they explored the open countryside they had to take shelter from the weather in an old cowshed. As they sat together waiting for the weather to clear, like Nicholas and Smike flung together on their first flight from Yorkshire, they talked to each other intimately for the first time, and were drawn together as friends, as they had never been in rehearsal. Back in rehearsal over the next few weeks their stage relationship also began to transform itself into a close bond of warmth and care. Greta Bridge did, it seemed, have one positive role to play in the Nicholas Nickleby story.

The last days of work in Newcastle concentrated on the other scenes in the first play not yet rehearsed. Relentlessly we worked through the beating of Smike, the flight from Yorkshire, and Kate's misfortunes at the Mantalinis. The one gap that remained was the scenes concerning the Crummles Theatre Company. Willoughby Goddard had contracted pneumonia, and we had to postpone the Crummles work completely until London, when we hoped he would be fully recovered. Though he thought at first he would recover, he finally had to withdraw from the production. With the gruelling weeks that lay ahead he felt he could no longer guarantee his fitness for the work. So after giving us all so much, he reluctantly became the next casualty from the project. With only a short period of rehearsal left we were fortunate in finding Graham Crowden to replace Willoughby just in time for the opening.

By the last few days in Newcastle, Trevor, John and I were exhausted. Rehearsals all day and meetings most of the night were wearing us out. Trevor and John were particularly tired as, after David and I left each evening, they continued talking and planning together until the early hours of the morning.

London
At Last

Nicholas discusses his new play with Mr Lenville (Christopher Ravenscroft)

In the few days that I had before rehearsals in London began, I had a little time to reflect on the work so far, in between washing clothes and trying to find somewhere to live.

Much of what we had done in Stratford and Newcastle had been new to most of us—the collective rehearsals; the multiple versions of each scene; the unusually close collaboration between writer and directors; the company improvisations; the storytelling techniques; and much more. But a cold eye cast over it would say that most of this had been done before elsewhere. Improvisatory rehearsal techniques had been used before, in many more sophisticated and advanced ways than we had attempted. Storytelling techniques had been explored in many different theatre companies, especially in fringe theatre and in the New York theatre of the sixties. Many of our conclusions had probably been reached by other actors and directors. So, I asked myself, what was so special about all this? It had something to do with the sheer scope of the project and the very specific location of it in a work by Dickens. There is little in Dickens that is intellectually or spiritually profound; that is not his concern. His focus on the way people are and the way that they live in society is more important to him. The work we had achieved so far was rooted in the strength of the social reality depicted by Dickens. The research and the early character explorations were geared deliberately to Dickens's world. The improvisatory work was limited to finding ways of translating descriptive prose into a theatrical language of communication that was as close as possible to his text. The solutions reached, although perhaps not totally original in themselves, were appropriate to the task of adapting an entire work of fiction. The project was unique for the sheer number of people involved and for the number and variety of storytelling techniques that were used. The decision to try and incorporate many different approaches stylistically, but all within one organically harmonious form, was becoming more and more the hallmark of what we were doing. The subject matter of a teeming, ever-moving, muscular Dickensian world hand in hand with the variety of forms and characters achieved by the large company was daily more exciting. True ensemble spirit was emerging as the central strength of the work. The painstaking early weeks of rehearsal began to have their effect on the company's attitude to the work and each other. It no longer seemed that it was all mammoth for its own sake, as I had sometimes suspected, but that it could not succeed without that all-embracing size.

It seemed to me then that the crucial question in the few weeks that were left was whether that diversity and completeness of intent could be sustained. As yet there was no binding physical centre to hold it all together as a single whole. It was still a series of fragments, sometimes brilliant, sometimes merely competent, and each part seemed strangely isolated and separate from the others.

John Napier had given us a start in the design of the set, but we had a long way to go. The world of Dickens, filled with its vast array of people swarming all around us, desperately needed a frame in which it could be contained. My greatest fear was that time would run out on us before that final, most elusive process could be completed. Now we had to go headfirst into the second play, which we still knew little about, and work on some scenes of the first play as yet only rehearsed once or twice. The task seemed daunting. We also had to finalise the structure of the second play which was already beginning to look too vast and unwieldy.

The company gathered again for rehearsal. Our new rehearsal home was in Floral Street in the heart of Covent Garden, next door to the Dance Centre, where a seemingly endless stream of energetic people, mainly female, passed by dressed in brightly-coloured tracksuits and white boots. The contrast between them and the pale, weary-looking faces that emerged from our somewhat seedier-looking entrance next door became marked.

There are windows all round the rooms in the building we used for our rehearsals, and a ceiling fitted with large glass panels. (I am told it was once a warehouse where bananas were stored.) There is one large room and one smaller, but most of the relevant proportions of the Aldwych stage can be represented in either. A storeroom packed full of old furniture and props, remnants and reminders of many past productions, make it a perfect rehearsal environment.

With those two rooms and various others nearby we were now able to rehearse in three spaces simultaneously, whenever possible. The logistics of it became a nightmare as John and I, who had the dubious honour of organising rehearsals, tried to organise a full day's work for each of the directors, although often it was only possible for John and Trevor to have enough actors for their scenes. We still did not know until halfway through various rehearsals who would be in them. It was not just named characters who were needed for each rehearsal of a given scene. Many scenes needed a large proportion of the company to comment and describe at key moments during the action. The stage management team began making up endless lists of names and characters and drawing up charts of possible double and treble rehearsal calls. They had already coped with far more than a normal rehearsal process. The original team of Phil Bassett as stage manager, David Proctor as deputy stage manager and Hilary Groves as assistant stage manager had come from Stratford to Newcastle and London with the company. In Newcastle, as the pressure built, they were aided by an additional assistant stage manager, Susan Miller, for a few weeks. But in London, the normal team of three, like everything else in the project, had to be expanded to cope with the mushrooming problems. Michael Townsend joined us as a second deputy stage manager and Simon Hooper replaced Susan as the second assistant stage manager. Like the directors and the designers, they worked closely together in the face of rapidly growing technical problems.

Using their lists and charts, they began to mobilise double or treble rehearsals as furniture and props were shuttled from one space to another. As they began to compile lists of furniture and props for each scene—although warned that everything would probably change again and again over the coming weeks—I calculated with John Caird the time needed for each scene to be rehearsed, and tried to announce ahead who would be with which director in which building. It only needed one actor to be late or one director to work behind schedule for the rest of the pack of cards to fall. Trevor Nunn, who often overran anyway, struggled in vain to keep to the schedule. We all miscalculated and erred in our plans as we grappled with new characters and scenes we had never rehearsed before.

After the delays caused by Willoughby Goddard's illness, work began again on the Crummles Theatre Company, still largely unrehearsed in Newcastle; and Graham Crowden gamely entered the spirit of the production. More than anything Trevor had looked forward to the Edgar and Shakespeare version of *Romeo and Juliet*. The first attempt, squeezed into a rushed rehearsal period, demonstrated to us some of the inherent problems. With the actors pretending to be actors acting, the ever-present danger of over-acting in the project came to a head.

Before the rehearsal a design for the Crummles performance had been agreed on. John Napier had offered Trevor a choice of designs from various nineteenth-century prints. The final design could well have been invented by Mr Crummles himself—a cut cloth of arches and in the background a painted scene of Verona. In front of the cut cloth, down some steps, would be the tomb area, represented by two simple bench-like objects covered with a cloth; one for Juliet, one for Tybalt. In one of the archways would be vertical prison bars, representing the way to look into the tomb from outside. Trevor and John Napier both knew well the problems of finding a credible tomb setting from their own previous experience of staging *Romeo and Juliet*.

Trevor continued further rehearsals of the scene, stressing the need to begin with a "straight" version, instead of a caricature performance. The actors played their parts in character for all they could, as though their acting careers in the Crummles Theatre Company depended on it. The obvious gags based on mock nineteenth-century histrionics were avoided, at least for a while. Trevor centred the key staging problems around a discovery in his own past production of *Romeo and Juliet*: the growing collections of swords and other implements that had to be discarded somewhere in the tomb as various characters enter and exit.

This second time through, with the basics of the design in place, the scene was slowly transformed into a comic masterpiece. The actors began to take their roles seriously within the confines of the Crummles characters they were playing. Everything, of course, in the Crummles Theatre Company's performance is a disaster, but the actors try very hard to get it right. In this way the scene also became to a degree an exercise in self-satire for the RSC.

The Crummles Theatre Company performing the Shakespeare/Edgar version of Romeo and Juliet

As the Crummles Theatre Company tripped over the scrapheap of swords and desperately propelled the performance to its end, before the drunken Wagstaff, Ben Kingsley, forgot too many more lines, the payoff of the earlier Crummles scenes occurred. But, although a comic climax to the sequences in the first play, it was not an ending in itself. There was a short further stage to go in order to include the full *Nicholas Nickleby* company in the ending of the first play. The Crummles Theatre Company performance was in itself too separate from the entire work of *Nicholas Nickleby*. Just as it had all begun with a full company sequence, so it should end with one. Also, although there was a clear upward build to the end of the first evening, it would be wrong to allow it all to end on an entirely happy note. The sufferings of Dotheboys Hall needed to be present somewhere at the end if the truth of the lost Dickens was to be held on to.

To this end, Stephen Oliver was asked to write a final after-curtain Crummles Company song that would in some way be merged with our own *Nicholas Nickleby* company ending to the play. He returned some days later with a pastiche of a nine-teenth-century patriotic song about the greatness of Victorian England—the sort of finale the Crummles Theatre Company would have used at the end of their performance.

England, arise:
Join in the chorus!
It is a new-made song you should be singing.
See in the skies,
Fluttering before us,
What the bright bird of peace is bringing.

See upon our smiling land,
Where the wealths of nations stand,
Where Prosperity and Industry walk ever hand in hand.

Where so many blessings crowd,
Tis our duty to be proud:
Up and answer, English yeomen, sing it joyfully aloud!

Evermore upon our country
God will pour his rich increase:
And victorious in war shall be made glorious in peace.

See each one do what he can
To further God's almighty plan:
The beneficence of heaven help the skilfulness of man.

Every garner filled with grain,
Every meadow blest with rain,
Rich and fertile is the golden corn that bears and bears again.

Where so many blessings crowd,
Tis our duty to be proud:
Up and answer, English yeomen, sing it joyfully aloud!

Evermore upon our country
God will pour his rich increase:
And victorious in war shall be made glorious in peace.

Stirring and rigorous, the satire of doggerel was the right thing to follow the *Romeo and Juliet* performance. In the middle of it all, Trevor proposed, would be Lila Kaye as Britannia, leading her troops in a song of patriotic celebration of nine-teenth-century England. Against this we would have to find a way of demonstrating in ironic counterpoint the less than glorious truth about Dickens's England, the England of Ralph Nickleby and Sir Mulberry Hawk and the suffering boys of Dotheboys Hall. In these ways we would merge the Crummles

Theatre Company with the entire *Nicholas Nickleby* company, who would at some point join in the song, to form an image of George Cruikshank's etching of the "British Beehive" of 1840. The play would therefore be complete theatrically and philosophically, although the continuing danger to Kate Nickleby left open the possibility of a driving reason for a new development of plot that would take Nicholas back to London.

Mr Crummles (Christopher Benjamin) bids farewell to Nicholas

Smike, Nicholas and Newman Noggs, watched by the company

PLAY TWO PROGRESSES

In these first six weeks at Floral Street the concentration was mostly on the second play. Many new scenes were rehearsed for the first time. The Mulberry Hawk plot began to develop as the characters of Sir Mulberry Hawk, played by Bob Peck, the young Lord Frederick Verisopht, Nick Gecks, and their two hangers-on Pyke and Pluck, Teddy Kempner and John Matshikiza, started to grow. The series of short scenes concerning them were constantly rewritten and re-rehearsed, first directed by John Caird and then passed backwards and forwards between him and me. We were particularly interested in the gradually changing relationship between Sir Mulberry and Lord Verisopht. In their first scene in the first play Lord Verisopht was clearly an affected dupe, standing by whilst Kate was tormented by Sir Mulberry. As the second play develops, his moral awareness is slowly awakened and his instinctive sense of honour forces him to see the corruption and evil in Sir Mulberry and his intentions towards Kate. More and more we began to feel, and Nick Gecks began to create, a young character about the same age as Nicholas, innocently led astray. The parallel to Nicholas becomes strongly evident as Lord Verisopht eventually sacrifices his own life in defence of Nicholas and his sister. Lord Verisopht's growing awareness of right and wrong corresponds with the declining fortunes of Sir Mulberry Hawk. David Edgar's money plot was the final link in that chain of connec-

Sir Mulberry Hawk nursing his wounds inflicted by Nicholas, with Lord Frederick Verisopht and Mr Pluck

tions as, in our version, the death of Lord Verisopht leads directly to the ruining of Sir Mulberry. According to Lord Verisopht's will his debts die with him and Sir Mulberry is finished financially as well as becoming a fugitive from the law for killing him in the duel. Bob Peck constructed in detail the character of Sir Mulberry Hawk, moving from glib confidence to anger and the final ironical mocking of Ralph Nickleby, who is also financially destroyed by Verisopht's death since he is the man responsible for all the young lord's debts. Nick Gecks fought hard against his natural instinct of making Verisopht too noble too soon, and traced a subtle development to the mature man aware of his guilt and prepared, inspired by Nicholas, to fight for what he believes to be right and honourable. Teddy

Susan Littler as Kate Nickleby

Kempner and John Matshikiza supported Nick and Bob Peck as well as they could, but were never quite happy with their very economically written characters of Pluck and Pyke.

Susan Littler meanwhile fought hard to give strength to Kate Nickleby. In Newcastle, on reading Kate's first scenes she had been very unhappy—hardly any dialogue or opportunity to develop a full character. We had still not fully solved the problems inherited from Dickens and Kate was shadowy and uncertain, though, as she argued with Sir Mulberry during his second manoeuvre to be alone with her at the house of the Wititterlies, she began to emerge as Nicholas's counterpart. The process went a stage further in her open argument with Ralph Nickleby whom she accuses of "selling her". Sue gave Kate strength and a sense of humour that lifted her out of a stock formula, but found the script did not give her far enough to go. Although, I believe, clearly miscast from the beginning, she did all that was possible to make a credible and interesting Kate; and some scenes, thanks to her ingenuity and ability, began to work well.

There were still completely new plots to work on that the actors had not yet seen—the arrival of the Cheeryble brothers and the plot concerning Arthur Gride and the marriage of Madeline Bray. In a nine-hundred-page novel that is serialised it is fair game to introduce an array of new characters and plots towards the end of the work, but on stage it is a dangerous process. After many hours in a theatre it is difficult to find interest in new additions to a complicated tangle of characters and events.

The Cheerybles are an important part of Dickens's framework. They represent the agents of good, using their wealth for the good of society. Through them Dickens betrays his basic middle-class belief in an affluent, industrial and humane society. He is not against the pursuit of wealth and the existence of gentlemen, on the contrary, he is in favour of it as long as honesty and compassion go hand in hand with it. The Cheerybles are his answer to Gride and Ralph, whose greed dictates how their wealth is used. When Nicholas refuses to marry Madeline, who is heir to property, because of the taint of money, in our version Frank Cheeryble is outraged at his generalised attack on wealth and points to his uncles, the Cheerybles, as the proof that money is not necessarily the root of evil.

However, although Dickens's Cheerybles are important to the story, as characters they are a problem. In the novel they are models of charity and goodness. They are quaint, eccentric men, but not highly developed comic creations: Dickens needed them to be perfect. We are never told on what their wealth is really founded, though there are vague allusions to mills and various export business concerns. What were conditions like for all their workers? We meet only a few of their employees, who are happy and benign. How did they manage to make enough profit to support their philanthropic pursuits without exploiting a work force in the first place? Where is their industrial base? Where do they come from themselves? Dickens avoids this territory. *Hard Times* may take on such questions, but not *Nicholas Nickleby*.

The Cheerybles had to be comic and yet sincere; the audience should laugh at their eccentricity, but not at their actions. They must also have a specific origin in order to provide a rich enough acting vehicle. Trevor, at the time of casting, suddenly provided the answer: "Why can't they be Welsh?". It made sense—the brothers describe in the novel how they journeyed to the capital, barefooted and penniless, to make their fortune. They might well have come from a poorer area like Wales. And the fiery Welsh temperament would make sense of their impulsive outbursts and stormy actions. With David Lloyd Meredith and Hubert Rees in the company, it all fitted into place.

David Edgar produced a draft scene for the four of us to read together. In spite of Trevor's terrible Welsh accent, the humour of the scene shone through. The Welsh character base worked, and David made the brothers understand each other so well that they shared thoughts and even sentences. They appeared like a comic duo. Two halves of one warm, colossal soul. It was difficult to judge how much of their verbosity could survive on stage

The Cheeryble brothers (Hubert Rees, sitting, and David Lloyd Meredith) interview Nicholas

without becoming too tedious, but on the whole David and the actors solved the major problems, though even after some cutting of the scenes the characters, to my mind, never quite made the full jump from the page to the stage. There was always something obsessively pure about the brothers that flawed the original writing of their characters in the novel and ultimately on the stage, however well they were acted. With Frank Cheeryble the success was perhaps greater; with the same accent and impulsive temperament as his uncles, but with a more recognisably real character, Frank stepped convincingly from the novel into the stage production. Frank, played by Christopher Ravenscroft, is close enough in nature to Nicholas to become the obvious partner for Kate Nickleby. Again, the parallels between the young men in the story became deeply marked in David Edgar's script. Smike, Nicholas, Lord Verisopht and Frank were all of a similar age, all brought up in drastically different circumstances but each finding his way to an understanding of himself and the world. Frank Cheeryble became another proof of Dickens's belief in the young.

It we had had a minor headache with Kate Nickleby, then we now had a migraine with Madeline Bray. In the novel, Nicholas's bride-to-be is delicate, pretty, ideal and boring. She has a thematic function and is there to be rescued by the gallant Nicholas. We searched the novel for clues to a more interesting character but found few. The only hope was to show her fortitude and determination in deciding to marry Gride in order to save her father from poverty, despair and certain death.

Walter Bray was not a lot easier to portray—an old, sick, angry man willing to sell his daughter to the ugly miser Arthur Gride in order to buy himself some physical comfort in his last years. As with Madeline, the problem was one of economy of writing. At such a late point in the story with an unconvincing, over-ingenious plot, the characters would have to be rapidly drawn and introduced. We fixed on the idea of keeping Bray in a wheelchair to be wheeled on and off by Madeline. In the novel, Bray lives in a debtor's house, and is looked after by a servant. However, we felt that as far as a contemporary audience was concerned, this would blur the picture of total poverty that was needed to convey the full extent of his and Madeline's plight. Similarly, we felt they actually needed to be seen in the prison, rather than a debtor's house.

Some of the short scenes seemed to work well: Juliet Hammond-Hill managed to find some sort of inner strength to Madeline in her refusal to give in to Nicholas's entreaties of love.

Walter Bray (Christopher Benjamin) and Madeline Bray (Lucy Gutteridge)

But on the whole, it was the least successful of the plots so far. The need for economy of writing also pushed us all into a series of short cuts that made it impossible for the actors fully to develop their characters.

The other character introduced at this point was old Peg Sliderskew, servant to Arthur Gride. David Edgar's creation, based on Suzanne Bertish's improvisation right back in the first weeks in Stratford, was an immediate success. He took the idea of an old hag with a Glaswegian accent to its logical conclusion and gave a brilliant vehicle for Suzanne Bertish, who eagerly exploited it. She now completed her extraordinary triple performance of the ugly, vain, young Fanny Squeers, the stunning Miss Snevellicci for the Crummles Theatre Company, and the repulsive old hag.

The most troubling area in this last plot section concerns the wedding day of Gride and Madeline. In the novel Dickens seems to have cornered himself. Nicholas has come on the wedding morning to beg Madeline not to marry Gride, but she will not break her promise. Dickens chooses a melodramatic device for this end—Bray suddenly dies:

> Gride hesitated: Ralph being by this time as furious as a baffled tiger made for the door, and attempting to pass Kate clasped her

*Suzanne Bertish as Fanny Squeers (top),
Miss Snevellicci (centre), and Peg
Sliderskew*

arm roughly with his hand. Nicholas with his eyes darting fire seized him by the collar. At that moment a heavy body fell with great violence on the floor above, and an instant afterwards was heard a most appalling and terrific scream.

They all stood still and gazed upon each other. Scream succeeded scream; a heavy pattering of feet succeeded; and many shrill voices clamouring together were heard to cry, "He is dead!"

"Stand off!" cried Nicholas, letting loose all the violent passion he had restrained till now, "if this is what I scarcely dare to hope it is, you are caught, villains, in your own toils."

He burst from the room, and darting upstairs to the quarter from whence the noise proceeded, forced his way through a crowd of persons who quite filled a small bed chamber, and found Bray lying on the floor quite dead, and his daughter clinging to the body.

We needed to find a simpler death that stood less chance of appearing accidentally comic. We also had to link the Hawk/Verisopht plot very closely and economically to the wedding morning. As the consequences of his financial plots come in on him, Ralph's world is collapsing all around him. In the novel, after Bray's death, Nicholas warns Ralph Nickleby that he is a finished man. Somehow Nicholas has heard that a business has collapsed and that Ralph has lost all his money. Dickens is vague on the subject and doesn't explain how Nicholas knows of what has happened. In our version, however, Verisopht's growth to moral awareness ends with his death that in turn financially ruins Hawk and Ralph Nickleby who is liable for all the young lord's debts. This tightening of the plot relates Ralph Nickleby's plots specifically to his own downfall.

Our problem was to weld this link together with the second plot that Ralph was involved in, concerning the marriage of Madeline to Gride.

The death of Bray marks another decline in Ralph's fortunes, and Nicholas is yet again there when a plot of Ralph's fails. Somehow, Nicholas had to hear the news about Verisopht's death. Trevor solved the problem by suggesting that Hawk himself could bring the news before his flight from England. The original scene that we rehearsed tried this, but the staging was awkward and the plot unclear. David rewrote the scene like the end of the film *The Graduate*. The wedding ceremony would actually be under way when Nicholas and Kate arrived to make a last ditch attempt to dissuade Madeline from going through with the marriage. As the reverend says: "If either of you know any impediment why ye may not be lawfully joined together in matrimony, ye do now confess it", Nicholas cries out: "Won't you, won't you confess it, Madeline?". Madeline wheels her father out so as not to hear what is going on. Before the argument between Ralph, Gride, Nicholas and Kate is complete, Sir Mulberry Hawk arrives, gun in hand, straight from the duel. He gloats at Ralph as he tells him about Verisopht's death and consequently Ralph's financial ruin and then he exits. Madeline comes in, crossing past Hawk in the doorway saying, "He's dead", referring to Bray who has died offstage. Hawk replies, "Oh, yes. He's dead. Indeed.", referring to Lord Frederick Verisopht. Thus the two plots merge and Madeline rejects Gride and exits with Kate. In one blow Ralph is destroyed on all sides and Nicholas leaves victorious.

Another new scene that had been written in Newcastle and was now worked on was known as SP4—or the death of Smike. In a discussion at the Swallow Hotel, Newcastle, Trevor had talked about it at great length and forcefully, asking David not to shrink from a full expression of the immensity of the sadness of Smike's death from any fear of being sentimental. Trevor seemed to feel more strongly about this area of the novel than anything hitherto. We all had to suspend our fear of sentimentality. For David, it was perhaps the greatest test to date. He did not say much at that meeting and kept his ideas a closely guarded secret until he presented Trevor, John and me with the scene.

The three of us quietly read David's script and were deeply moved. We were also impressed by the technical brilliance of the devices that he had created for the scene. It was to be one of the few scenes in which not a single word was changed. After a very simple introduction to the setting, back at Nicholas's and Kate's home village, out in the meadows where they used to play as children, Smike lies down to rest whilst Nicholas and Kate talk of their respective loves for Madeline Bray and Frank Cheeryble. Then, David's invention took over from the novel. Smike, using the words of the apothecary from *Romeo and Juliet* learnt in the Crummles Theatre Company, calls out, "Who calls? Who calls so loud?". As he repeats the line Nicholas realises that Smike is urging him to reply in words from *Romeo and Juliet*:

NICHOLAS: Come hither, man. I see that thou art poor. Hold, there is forty ducats. Let me have—
SMIKE: Such mortal drugs I have, but Mantua's law—Is—is—
NICHOLAS: Oh, Smike—
SMIKE: Is death to any he that utters them.
   (Prompting): Art thou so bare—?
NICHOLAS: Art thou so bare and full of wretchedness,
       And fearest to die? Famine is in thy cheeks,
       Need and oppression starveth in thy eyes.
       Contempt and—

Smike

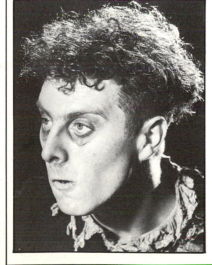

Nicholas and Smike

SMIKE: No. No, I don't fear to die. My will consents.

(NICHOLAS turns round to embrace SMIKE, who throws his arms round NICHOLAS'S neck to stop himself collapsing.)

SMIKE/*con.* You know, I think, that if I could rise up again, completely well, I wouldn't want to, now.

(SMIKE looking over NICHOLAS'S shoulder at KATE):

For nothing—can be ill, if she be well.

NICHOLAS: Then she is well, and nothing can be ill.

(Pause)

Her body sleeps in Capel's monument.

(Pause)

But her immortal part with angels lives.

SMIKE: Is it. E'en so. I see a garden. Trees and happy children's faces. And her body sleeps. Light on the faces. Living with the angels. Dreamt my lady came and found me. dead. Such happy dreams.

(He pulls himself up to whisper in NICHOLAS'S ear. Then, out loud to KATE):

I'm going home. Who calls. Who calls so loud?

(SMIKE is still. NICHOLAS realises he is dead. He picks him up in his arms. He turns to KATE. He is crying.)

NICHOLAS: He said—I think you know.

(Pause. KATE can say nothing.)

NICHOLAS/*cont.* And then he said he was in Eden.

Thus Smike is reconciled happily to death, in his last words expressing his love for Kate. David took the *Romeo and Juliet* theme from the first play to a conclusion with the death of Smike. From the helpless, crushed victim at the beginning of the first play, who could hardly talk or think, Smike has grown and developed into a thinking and loving human being, capable of complex thoughts and emotions. With love and care the destroyed creature of Dotheboys Hall has come a long way on his journey through friendship with Nicholas and through laughter at the Crummles Theatre Company to love for Kate. His death is therefore a most bitter and ironical blow at the same moment of final growth. Like the death of Cordelia in *King Lear*, the shadow of Smike's death still remains at the end of the work. We too wanted a way to remember that at the end of the second play.

The penultimate scene to Play Two was also explored for the first time. From a very early point in the project we had talked about possible endings to the production. The Christmas theme had been there from nearly the beginning, but David Edgar had also talked about his image of something less settled and comfortable. In the novel Dickens refers to the boys escaping from Dotheboys Hall, after Squeers has been sent to Australia. David suggested that the collapse of the school and escape of the pupils could be an important image near or at the end of the play. He wrote a short scene that described the boys in revolt against Mrs Squeers and Fanny, violently destroying everything in the building before escaping. Playing on the words "break-up" at end of term, he depicted the scene as a riot of revenge. He then linked this through to the last scene of the play, in which the entire company sings "God Rest Ye Merry, Gentlemen", by the device of a single boy sitting alone on the stage. He originally called this pathetic figure "The Other Smike"; the idea was that he had become a replacement drudge in the school after Smike's departure. Then, whilst everyone else is celebrating the harmony and happy ending of Christmas, this figure is still there as a reminder that all is not well in the world. Nicholas, alone, sees him outside in the cold and goes and takes him in his arms. Thus, the last movements of the play take Nicholas back to Yorkshire to finish the process he had begun at Dotheboys Hall, and at the very end shows him aware of what has yet to be done.

The roles that grew most during those four to six weeks were those of Edward Petherbridge and Roger Rees. Edward had become increasingly unhappy with the way Noggs had been written. He was frustrated at the constant reduction of his key scenes in the novel to odd half lines and monosyllabic utterances. David Edgar argued that this economy of speech was one of the hallmarks of Noggs's character. Edward felt that a major character was not being fully represented in the script. A series of confrontations took place and acrimonious notes went to and fro. Edward was challenged to indicate specific grievances and he did. The directors began to feel that Edward had a case. On careful examination of the script we could see that one or two brilliant observations in Dickens had been omitted. On the

whole they were short in length, but full of key significance in relation to character. Edward had particularly fixed on moments of rich eccentricity such as when, almost caught reading the letter from Ralph to Gride:

> "Do you see anything particular, Mr Noggs?" said Arthur, trying to follow the direction of Newman's eyes—which was an impossibility, and a thing no man had ever done.
> "Only a cobweb," replied Newman.
> "Oh! Is that all?"
> "No," said Newman. "There's a fly in it."
> "There are a good many cobwebs here," observed Arthur Gride.
> "So there are in our place," returned Newman; "and flies, too."
> Newman appeared to derive great entertainment from this repartee, and to the great discomposure of Arthur Gride's nerves produced a series of sharp cracks from his finger-joints, resembling the noise of a distant discharge of small artillery. Arthur succeeded in finishing his reply to Ralph's note, nevertheless, and at length handed it over to the eccentric messenger for delivery.

David finally incorporated some of the proposals into the script and everyone was satisfied. From that moment on, Edward dropped his resistance to the script and began to create perhaps the most detailed and brilliant characterisation of any in the production. Carefully exploiting all Newman Noggs's eccentricities, turns of phrase, cracking finger-joints and crossed eyes, he built up an extraordinary character, yet balanced it by bringing out the reality behind the outwardly crazy form. It was a Dickensian portrait with a totally credible, recognisable human quality and warmth. Although some of his speeches might have been curtailed, Edward built from them an unforgettable characterisation that hovered on the brink of caricature but never fell in. David Edgar's defence of the economy of language proved to be as right as Edward's insistence on reinstating critical moments of the script. Trevor felt that Edward had been challenged not to confuse length of utterance with significance or centrality of character. He believed that Edward then began to work, where before he was evaluating.

Whilst Edward began to create Newman Noggs, Roger Rees battled on with Nicholas Nickleby. Having been given the unenviable task of playing a hero half his age, Roger had immediately thrown himself energetically into the job. Nicholas is not at first sight a particularly attractive role for an actor such as Roger, who has now declared Nicholas to have been his last juvenile lead. (But of course, he forgets Hamlet when he declares this.) Roger is incapable of doing anything half-heartedly. His immense energy and enthusiasm is contagious to all around

Edward Petherbridge as Newman Noggs

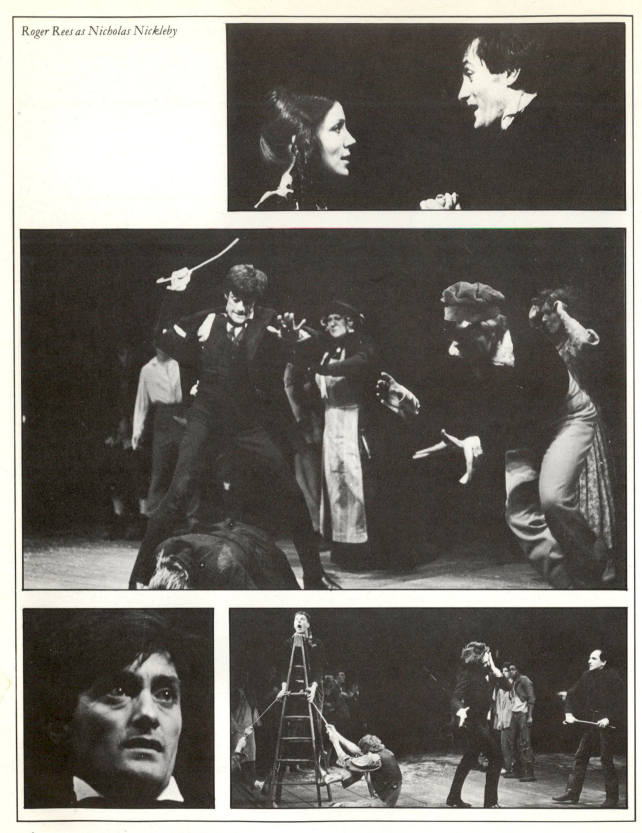

Roger Rees as Nicholas Nickleby

him and he is the perfect company leader. From the early Stratford days of the project onwards he had been at the centre of all we did. He is probably the best liked acting member of the RSC, and uses his instinctive sense of tact and diplomacy to promote his beliefs without offending anyone. His charismatic personality draws people to him from all directions. He has numerous fans who collect after each performance at the stage door and write him countless letters, all of which he answers. Roger is also the perfect actor to direct. Whilst always offering his own inventive thoughts and ingenious interpretations, he is quick to respond to outside direction. He thrives on notes and criticism and is always keen to try other ways of working. His ability to listen to an actor and share an acting process is the same as his attitude to all those around him. Roger is a great listener to all his colleagues and the public who come to see him.

But there is another side to Roger, not so often seen. Underneath the generous exterior is a very tough, determined man. Although always listening to others, he has a sharp, critical and sometimes sardonic sense of humour. He is quick to identify the weakness in others and is able to locate people's foibles precisely and fix upon the absurdity of certain situations with a lightning wit that can often sting. Roger knows what he wants and how, patiently, to get it. His love of many of the RSC's traditions and methods of work go hand in hand with a healthy irreverence for the rest of it when he believes it to be stale or insufficient. He is deeply critical of directors and actors who do not nurture carefully enough their productions once they have opened. Roger continues working on a role throughout a production.

It is these resilient and tougher sides of Roger's nature that help to make him such a fine actor. He understands violence and anger as well as the brighter sides of characters' natures that come so easily to him. Roger and the directors knew that he had to find those darker moments in Nicholas in order to discover the full, complex, imperfect hero described by Dickens The young Dickens, at twenty-six years, was disturbed and angered by the injustices around him. Nicholas too is an angry young man of his time who at moments of high emotional strain suddenly has recourse to violence. Nicholas viciously attacks Squeers when he beats the helpless Smike. Nicholas does not "somehow come between them" (like the conscientious objector who was asked by the army tribunal what he would do if he saw his sister being raped) but goes a stage further and beats Squeers violently to the ground.

He had scarcely spoken when Squeers, in a violent outbreak of wrath and with a cry like a howl of a wild beast, spat upon him, and struck him a blow across the face with his instrument of torture, which raised up a bar of livid flesh as it was inflicted. Smarting with the agony of the blow, and concentrating into that one moment all his feelings of rage, scorn, and indignation, Nicholas sprang upon him, wrested the weapon from his hand, and, pinning him by the throat, beat the ruffian till he roared for mercy.

The boys—with the exception of Master Squeers, who, coming to his father's assistance, harassed the enemy in the rear—moved not hand or foot; but Mrs Squeers, with many shrieks for aid, hung on to the tail of her partner's coat and endeavoured to drag him from his infuriated adversary; while Miss Squeers, who had been peeping through the keyhole in expectation of a very different scene, darted in at the very beginning of the attack, and after launching a shower of inkstands at the usher's head, beat Nicholas to her heart's content, animating herself at every blow with the recollection of his having refused her proffered love, and thus imparting additional strength to an arm which (as she took after her mother in this respect) was at no time one of the weakest.

Nicholas, in the full torrent of his violence, felt the blows no more than if they had been dealt with feathers; but becoming tired of the noise and uproar, and feeling that his arm grew weak besides, he threw all his remaining strength into half a dozen finishing cuts, and flung Squeers from him with all the force he could muster. The violence of his fall, precipitated Mrs Squeers completely over an adjacent form, and Squeers, striking his head against it in his descent, lay at his full length on the ground, stunned and motionless.

Although Dickens is careful here to make Squeers strike Nicholas first, his excessively violent response is described with great sympathy. The angry Nicholas strikes back in a moment when all his frustrations, hatred and disgust for Squeers and Dotheboys Hall culminate in one act of violence. Dickens defends his violent young hero in his second preface of 1848: "If Nicholas be not always found to be blameless or agreeable, he is not always intended to appear so. He is a young man of an impetuous temper and of little or no experience and I saw no reason why such a hero should be lifted out of nature".

Later in the novel, Nicholas is outraged when overhearing Sir Mulberry Hawk speak disrespectfully about Kate, his sister. After challenging Sir Mulberry to answer to his words and scorned by Sir Mulberry, Nicholas waits for him to leave the coffee-house. Nicholas follows Sir Mulberry and grabs the rein of his cabriolet. The horses rear up violently, threatening to upturn the carriage. As Sir Mulberry Hawk strikes Nicholas, Nicholas fights back: "Nicholas gained the heavy handle and with it laid open one side of his antagonist's face from the eye to the lip".

For Roger and the four of us it was a critical area of the character of Nicholas. Nicholas was not the perfect melodrama hero and we all agreed that such scenes should be included at all costs. The image of Nicholas's fist also became the dominant image for publicity for the production, featured in Ginni Moo-Young's brilliant poster. A strident, defiant, aggressive defender of truth, not a cut-out, gentle, passive hero.

Roger eagerly built on those aspects of Nicholas's character and merged them with his earlier work on the simple, innocent Nicholas found at the opening of the story. Carefully watching the younger actors at work, Roger noticed, as he put it, their "spiky" movements, and tried to move in a similar way. The narrative passages in the novel also helped as Roger could speak as Nicholas in a wry, detached manner about the events he was involved in. Roger could therefore use the voice of Dickens as well as of Nicholas. Again, Roger exploited well this side of Nicholas that could comment and mock as well as be intensely involved in the situation. By the end of the six weeks in London, Roger had constructed a dynamic and complex character.

Perhaps the individually most exciting rehearsal was an afternoon working on the creation of a stagecoach. We knew that we wanted to represent in some way Nicholas's departure for Yorkshire. Trevor had argued early on in the project that it must be done by an imaginative device of some kind, relying on the actors and the materials around them on stage. He was against the use of any additional complex stage-machinery. His idea was to build a stagecoach on stage in direct sight of the audience. John Napier had suggested that it could be constructed on one of the moving trucks so that it could be seen to leave the stage.

When the rehearsal began most of the company were sceptical as Trevor asked them to find a way of making the vehicle. Bob Peck was particularly difficult and continually challenged Trevor to be more explicit about what he wanted. But as the afternoon went by a remarkable change of mood occurred in the room as an extraordinary creation emerged. Bob Peck was now in the vanguard of the enthusiastic company collecting props and furniture from all around the rehearsal room. They began to build up a pile of skips and suitcases on top of tables and other objects capable of supporting heavy weights. A group of actors piled in and on the construction, many feet up in the air. Refined by Trevor, it had indeed become a stagecoach. Later, when rehearsed until it could be built at high speed, it was tried out on set, on top of the truck. From the very first preview performance onwards it always received an ovation as a large group of the actors pushed the stagecoach off, with Nicholas and the other passengers waving farewell. Stylistically, the rehearsal was an important achievement as it proved how collective imaginations could achieve startling effects with the human and material resources already at our command. Invention was our greatest ally.

Whilst some of these key characterisations were developing and new scenes were moving forward, the directors still had many problems. With the opening not far away, David Edgar had much rewriting still to go and numerous scenes had still not yet ever been rehearsed. Although we were rehearsing as much as possible, many scenes had only as yet been very superficially skimmed through. The structure of the second play was still in great confusion. We had far too much material and no way as yet of fitting it all together that made any sense.

However, we were ready to put Play One together, and to begin plotting the physical life of the production. We began at the beginning and started to imagine the actual physical staging requirements of each scene and each scene change. Carefully, every movement of furniture was plotted and an actor allocated to move it on and off. The positions of each object were fixed and recorded by stage management. In particular, much time was taken refining Trevor's stagecoach and the building of it. Finally, it could be built in just a few minutes with every one of the large numbers of people on stage given exact duties. By the end of the day we had only managed to reach the tea-party scene, about halfway through the Dotheboys Hall sequence. But the day's work proved invaluable later, and now, at last, the fragments were beginning to come together.

The final part of this moulding together process was to be the first run-through on Play One, from beginning to end. Now, we all felt that it was taking shape at last. All the company became increasingly involved and enthusiastic as the pieces unmistakably merged into an enthralling story. The actors not performing sat watching the others and the response was electric. The humorous scenes were greeted with howls of laughter as the company realised how very funny it could be. The quiet, intense moments were followed in concentrated silence. A major breakthrough had taken place and morale was high as the fruits of months of work were displayed. We were all delighted and surprised at how advanced much of it was. Stephen Oliver had had the opportunity to sort out many problems and David Hersey, lighting designer, had sat surrounded by charts and plans taking detailed notes. The only major worry was to see how we could come close to the same state of preparedness with Play Two.

AT THE RAINBOW THEATRE

An average production budget for a main house show at the RSC is in the region of thirty thousand pounds. That figure includes all costs except the payment of the acting company and regular staff. Any overtime payments or extra specialist help, such as a fight arranger or choreographer, also comes from this budget.

Nicholas Nickleby, originally conceived at a time of financial crisis, was morally and financially obliged to stay as a relatively low-cost production. In the event, when we realised how it was in fact equivalent to two very large-scale productions, it was budgeted at around sixty thousand pounds, like any other pair of shows. John Napier had been encouraged to break many design rules and create a radical, anarchic structural design. Now, at a design meeting at the Aldwych Theatre a few weeks after the beginning of London rehearsals, we heard that the estimated cost of building the set was far too high to be approved. Many drastic changes would have to take place to bring it within budget. John Napier refused to compromise his design and offered his resignation from the project. He was weary of always having his work altered and cut down by the RSC. It was to be all or nothing. How could he be asked to break every rule on such a vast scale and then be told to reduce it again?

To provide the direct contact between actors and audience in the stalls and dress circle that Trevor had wanted, John had proposed building a runway around the front of the dress circle that had to be welded and supported by scaffolding in the auditorium. This in itself could only be achieved at great expense. The platform that would thrust out right through the front rows of the stalls necessitated removing a number of seats; this meant a loss of box office income. All this, in addition to the high cost of timber all over the design, amounted to an enormous basic cost. The sheer scale and complexity of building suggested a high overtime bill for constructing it quickly: the crew would have to work at night and outside contractors would be needed —otherwise performances of the plays already in the repertory would have to be cancelled (at great financial loss) to give us more time to build the set.

The hire bill for the costumes also looked ominously high—a few hundred characters needed to be created, and only a few costumes would have to be made. In addition, there were as yet the unknown factors of wigs, which could add more to the final bill. There was little room to manoeuvre because the whole conception of use of costumes, furniture and props was already geared to maximum economy. Full dress costumes were already being avoided, trousers were to stay the same whilst jackets were to be swapped over. Furniture was already being collected from cheap sources and some of the junk we normally reserved for rehearsal was to be employed in the final productions.

It was stalemate. John refused to compromise his set and the RSC could not provide extra cash. For a few days, more detailed estimates were made. Then there was a breakthrough.

John agreed to make some modifications to the set. Nothing drastic was altered, but bit by bit he took out anything at all that could be disposed of. He and Dermot found a way to reinstate the displaced seats elsewhere in the theatre. The original extra change of stage level he had wanted at the front of the stage was taken out. Finally, and most important of all, we decided to try and cut down the time needed to build the set in the Aldwych Theatre. To this end we accepted an idea that not only solved the major financial problem but also changed the course of all our work on *Nicholas Nickleby*. We planned to build a working version of the set a few weeks in advance of the opening of the production in a warehouse somewhere in London. John Napier and Dermot would then have time for modifications and practical alterations before the set was put up at the Aldwych. At the same time, the directors and the acting company would actually rehearse on the set so that we could discover much more about what we were doing. We were anticipating potentially severe physical problems with the set both for actors and stage crew.

With all these agreements it would be just possible to squeeze everything in within the budget. Simon Opie, production manager for the Aldwych, set about trying to find a space for our experimental set-building. A few weeks later he announced that he had booked the Rainbow Theatre in Finsbury Park—the London home of rock concerts—which happened to be empty for a week, having failed to lease a disused printing works near the Aldwych. This change of plan would save half the entire cost of building the set. We would now be able to build with our own crew, instead of outside contractors.

So, after six weeks of rehearsal in London, on 18 May, the stage crew and builders began to move in to the Rainbow Theatre. After two days of work, the acting company moved in on the afternoon of 20 May. By now our company were used to moving from one rehearsal space to another in Stratford, Newcastle and London, but the Rainbow Theatre was the most extraordinary rehearsal space of all. Built in 1930 as a gigantic cinema and variety theatre called the Astoria, it still retains all its original splendour. The generous foyer on two levels is brightly carpeted and decorated in rust and green throughout. All around are extraordinary reminders of the fantasy designs of the period, based on a Moroccan theme. Inside the vast auditorium is an extremely wide stage. On the high ceiling, towering above the auditorium seats is a planetarium sky complete with galaxies of twinkling lights like stars. On this stage the crew had erected the skeleton of John Napier's set. Although enormous by Aldwych Theatre standards, it looked quite lost in the middle of the Rainbow stage. The dress circle catwalk from the model had to be built across the front of the stage as the circle seats at the Rainbow Theatre are miles away from the edge of the stage. Trevor, John and I went along a day before the actors to see the progress. We climbed eagerly over the set, discovering it like an adventure playground, while John Napier and Dermot Hayes stood miserably by, angry and dismayed. So many corners had had to be cut on costs and time that the entire structure was, John Napier told us, unsound. While for us a hitherto abstract concept had suddenly been made physical, the designers saw an inadequate and unsafe version of what they had already clearly imagined concretely beforehand. However much the directors analysed and understood the sketches and, indeed, the model, the structural features and safety problems of a full-size three-dimensional set had been a partial mystery to us.

Whilst Trevor organised with John what had to be done,

Ralph Nickleby introduces himself to Miss La Creevy

John Caird and I clambered all over the set finding out the danger areas. We were aware now of how dangerous such a set could be—with an unsteady bridge up high in the air, large wooden trucks on wheels and steps and stairs everywhere, there seemed to be hazards wherever we looked. From past experience of difficult sets, Trevor feared that a few actors would refuse to climb up on the structure when requested in case of accidents. We knew that it would take time to achieve all these changes and the cast were due in the next day. We had to hope the company would continue rehearsal with care, whilst the changes gradually took place.

We planned to divide the week's work into two distinct halves, with the first days on Play One and then Play Two. We intended to run through both plays technically with the set in as much detail as possible. This way we felt we would speed up the final work in the Aldwych just before the opening night.

That evening, Trevor, John and I began our preparation for the next day's work. Trevor was particularly concerned about furniture and props. So much of the materials and furniture were recycled throughout the two plays from scene to scene that meticulous organisation would be needed. We wanted to discover the most dynamic, inventive, and surprising way of using each object as we constantly re-employed the familiar.

Every item was to have a specific home on the set, on a hook or in a corner or on top of another object. That way each actor would learn immediately where to put a given object at a given time. Each chair, for example, might be used in ten or eleven different scenes; and each time a different actor might have to place it on stage or remove it at the end of one of those scenes. With dozens of objects and over forty actors moving about, let alone the two enormous trucks on wheels, chaos and danger could soon result. We spent hours calculating the best positions for each object for the first few scenes and we drew up with stage management an inventory and map, following on from the work begun a week earlier at Floral Street.

Trevor was insistent on this process. He needed to feel that our rehearsal process was being constructed and organised, physically and mentally. During the long months of rehearsals, he had had very few serious disagreements with John Caird, but the question of advance planning and directorial homework had been one of those rare topics of dispute. At a point in our work some weeks earlier Trevor had become increasingly frustrated by the necessity for unprepared and unconsidered direction in rehearsal. Sometimes the directors had to begin rehearsal on

The company explore the set for the first time at the Rainbow Theatre

scenes we had never read until a few hours before. With unclear ideas of specific settings, scenes had sometimes to be re-rehearsed a few days apart with instructions to the actors changed. Trevor despaired at running unplanned rehearsals and disliked being seen to be fickle about practical decisions, although he still directed brilliantly under those conditions. John Caird was less concerned about these particular problems, and tended by instinct to prepare less for specific rehearsals anyway. Trevor's frustrations at what for him was an unnatural working method had led to heated exchanges. Trevor was now keen to restore a carefully prepared system of work in order to guide us through the final hurdles of production planning. The meticulous physical preparations were part of this process.

As we were finally about to leave the Rainbow Theatre that first night, I stood at the back of the stalls and looked for a moment at the amazing structure on the stage. With glaring lights on the set for John Napier, Dermot and the crew to begin work overnight, it glowed like a power station in the dark. In triumph and ecstasy a black and white theatre cat leapt joyously from pole to pole across the scaffolding. He had found the perfect set. I hoped the acting company would share his sentiments.

On the afternoon of 20 May the actors arrived. I've never seen a company so excited about a new set. The more adventurous members of the company eagerly ran and climbed all over it. Some of the more cautious actors walked about touching and admiring it. In spite of the obvious problems they were all thrilled. Trevor gave, as Phil Basset the stage manager put it, a wonderful over-the-top speech about care and safety and the unique opportunity that we now had and the exciting possibilities that were ahead. Morale soared to an all-time high.

We began with the opening scene and started to work our way through the play. Although one of the trucks was not yet installed we had enough of the set and props to commence. We bypassed any moments that were physically impossible to work out with the incomplete set. By the end of the afternoon we had only just got through the opening narration and part of the first scene, and the company had to break for a performance of *The Merry Wives of Windsor*. Some excellent progress had been made in beginning to understand what John Napier had really given us. We were delighted and relieved that the truck could be moved easily without too much manpower. At one point in rehearsals we had feared needing large numbers of people to heave off the trucks at each scene change. Yet, at the same time, as

John Napier had advised us many weeks before, the length of time it took and the noise it made warned us that we should continue to use the trucks sparingly.

That night we planned more furniture positions and plotted more maps, and resolved to work a lot faster the next day.

But the next day progress was still very slow. Each scene setting took hours to organise, even with carefully prepared plans. New physical problems arose continually as entrances and exits were changed, furniture altered and staging modified. By the end of the day only a few scenes had been finished. When we met late that night we knew that our schedule for the week was already wrecked. There was no way in which we could complete our plans to go through the entirety of both plays at the Rainbow Theatre. We would be lucky if we got through the first play at the rate we were going. But there was nothing else to do: we had to complete the process we had embarked upon. Trevor was determined not to cut any more corners—his instinct for order had taken over from the intellectual discussion about the use of our time. Although John and Trevor were in many ways good together as a team of directors, there was one problem. Their directorial relationship required that John should challenge Trevor's attitudes towards and plans for rehearsal. He had always required that of John and was pleased with the way it had worked. Often, in important ways for the project, Trevor had rethought or changed course as a consequence of what John had criticised. However, I also believe that Trevor is at his best when trusting his own instinct, even when that sometimes goes against logic and consistency. Many times during the *Nicholas Nickleby* rehearsals I had been impressed by Trevor's directorial instinct at work; when it was restricted too often he seemed to me unhappy and stifled in what he was doing. Now, he was beginning to operate more and more in his own natural rhythms and by his own instinctive methods. The technical process would be thorough at all costs; whatever else happened over the next few weeks Trevor knew we would have the security of having undergone that process.

By the third day John Napier and Dermot Hayes had made great changes to the set. It was much more stable and the finish of iron gratings and Victorian metalwork had begun to be arranged all over it. Modern scaffolding was slowly being transformed into industrial nineteenth-century England—and wooden planks and ropes covered the modern metallic structure.

Although the work was still slow we were becoming more familiar with the set—its advantages and drawbacks. We were

overleaf: Nicholas and Smike on their way to Portsmouth

learning to work with the trucks and beginning to feel more confident of how to use them. All the time we were conscious of the risks of accidents and elaborate precautions were taken.

The next days there were slow and hard as we painstakingly worked our way through the first play on stage, whilst scenes from Play Two were rehearsed in odd corners all over the Rainbow Theatre. Each day the routine remained unchanged—rehearsal all day and evening with a few breaks for the actors. Trevor, John and I continued right through, using the actors' breaks to work through text, music cues, furniture plots and numerous other plans and details of the work. As we were unable to stop in order to go out for food, Hilary Groves fed us on home-made cold food banquets whilst the actors strolled around Finsbury Park.

In the late evenings when the company had broken, we had to continue with the planning and organising for the next day. As we progressed towards the end of the first play our growing familiarity with the set helped us to plan more accurately the work ahead. We pushed harder and harder each day until near the end of the week the end was in sight. Trevor and John were even more tired than me as they continued working together after our meetings until the early hours at Trevor's house in Hampstead.

Still not there, we pleaded with Simon Opie and the production team to allow us some extra hours on the last day that was scheduled for the crew to move everything out. Reluctantly they agreed and we spent a final few hours on the set on 28 May, almost reaching the end of Play One. And then, after lunch, we returned to Floral Street.

That week at the Rainbow Theatre had completely transformed our fragments into a whole—as far as Play One was concerned. Only a little work had been done on Play Two. The moulding together of the scenes on the set had been a critical process at that stage in the work. David Edgar had had the opportunity to work on numerous small rewrites, necessitated by the pressures of physical problems encountered on stage. Stephen Oliver had been able to calculate more accurately timings for musical scores. Trevor, John and I had been able to adapt theory to practical reality. What was disturbing was the sheer length of it all, and the fact that the second play had hardly been touched. Eight days away was the first public performance of Play One. Five days later Play Two would also open to the public, and we still did not have a physical production for it.

We completely froze all work on Play One and relentlessly

worked our way through scenes from Play Two—some of which still had not been rehearsed in any form. Learning from our experience of scene changes and moving trucks at the Rainbow we simplified the staging of that second play as much as possible, to have less furniture and setting, more use of the actors as a whole company on stage to create the atmosphere. We had always known that the nature of the two plays would be different. Play One has a clear structure and plot: first half Dotheboys Hall and the Mantalinis, second half Crummles Theatre Company and Sir Mulberry Hawk. Nicholas learns about the world, befriends Smike; Kate goes out to work and is pursued by Sir Mulberry Hawk. The movement on the whole is to one of celebration and joy with the Crummles Theatre Company and their performance of *Romeo and Juliet*. The second play is a more unwieldy and complex structure with multiple plots and a central tale of suspense and intrigue. Running through the centre of it is an involved money plot gradually connecting together the different sections. Under-rehearsed and under-prepared as it was, it had a sprawling quality that needed a firm structure if it was ever to be properly contained.

The problems reached a crisis point, with the opening only a few weeks away. In hours of meetings with David we had not found a solution to the structural problems. In particular, we were unable to find a satisfactory way of introducing the new Gride plot and connecting it to the Nicholas plot, at such a late point in the play. As a last resort Trevor and John decided to get away from London for a weekend to Christminster. They worked for thirty-six hours without sleep, analysing the possibilities. Trevor feared cancellation if the answer could not be found. They drew up four different versions of the play and finally arrived at a structure that made sense. At the same time as offering a solution to the Gride plot problem it also took forty-five minutes of playing time off the show. They presented the new plan as a *fait accompli* to David and me, and we set about trying to make it work.

Whilst we rehearsed at full speed John Napier ploughed ahead with the costume fittings, and the set was handed over to Dermot to finish. John had begun fittings as soon as rehearsals had started in London. By the end of the week at the Rainbow, the whole of Play One had been costumed, but only part of Play Two. It was a long and difficult process, and John was only able to fit two or three costumes in a day. We had to work out rehearsal schedules that allowed John to have the actors he needed.

John had calculated carefully the amount of time needed for

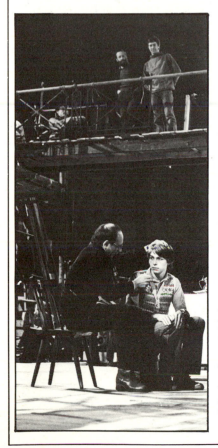

Squeers (Ben Kingsley) talks to his newest recruit, Belling

John Napier fits the Infant Phenomenon (Julie Peasgood) with her costume

so many costumes and had realised how close it would be. He organised his team of assistants to go through every page of the novel and record every single costume detail mentioned by Dickens. Working on the assumption that the various illustrators had similarly worked from textual evidence he also asked them to collate as many different illustrations as possible. He asked all the actors to write down for him their own feelings about their characters and what they might wear, as he was too busy to be able to watch many rehearsals. All this material was gathered in a large book into which he began adding polaroid photographs of each character as he or she was fitted. With this material as a starting point he then improvised costumes on the actors in countless hours of fittings among many thousands of Victorian clothes in costumiers in London. He showed each photograph to Trevor for comment as he went along. Miraculously, few changes were needed. These pictures were also about the only way that every costume detail would be remembered. With the pressure of rehearsal it had been hard to release actors for long fitting sessions. Now we had to release them to speed up the process, even if rehearsals suffered.

The computation of actors, characters and scenes ran to hundreds and John was unable to see the company in any chronological order, yet he managed to conceive in his imagination far more than any illustrator ever had to. We saw when we staged the scenes in costume that he had used remarkable instinct and calculation to produce an extraordinary control of his colour palette. Whole scenes contained complete colour designs of great beauty and relevance. John had also responded in the designs and colours to the textual demands of central or background character focus.

Whilst John worked relentlessly on the costumes, Stephen Oliver continued preparing his scores. The musical strategy had been established many weeks before, and we had established from the onset that music would be an integral part of the production. Trevor had asked Stephen to create certain musical themes that could represent particular feelings, attitudes or characters. These could be repeated at key points during the two evenings. Sometimes, the music might be used under dialogue, as in films, to enhance emotions almost subliminally, and at other times, as in most stage productions, to cover entrances and exits and aid transitions from one scene to another. In addition there would be the set piece songs and the Italian opera visited by the Wititterlies and Kate Nickleby.

Stephen played through what he had written so far and Trevor

The opera

was delighted. There was a theme called "The Farm" to represent the country and associations of the Nickleby family at home in Devon—a melodious piece based on a simple tune; a "London" theme, spirited and capable also of being played melancholically at a slow tempo—representing money and wealth side by side with poverty (opposite in every way to the "Farm" theme); a "Farewell" song, to be sung by Mrs Grudden, and to be played without words at other points in the script; a "Mulberry Hawk" theme—bluesey, jazzy, evocative of cigar smoke-filled clubs; a "Milliners" theme that was later expanded to become chase music, for Mr Mantalini's run around the dress circle walkway; a "Smike" theme—sad and strange sounding; and a "Wedding" theme, based on a setting to a psalm. That was vital for the important associations of marriage in the play. We also heard Stephen's mock Donizetti opera which we did use, at a reduced length, and his operetta for the Crummles Theatre Company, which we didn't.

At our earlier meeting Stephen had asked Trevor to define a style of music that he wanted. Trevor had asked for music that invoked the period of the production rather than anything recognisably twentieth century. I was a little disappointed that there would not be room for what is genuinely Stephen's own style of writing music, which he describes as "twentieth-century idiom". Trevor indicated clearly that he wanted something more conventional and lyrical, and John Caird showed how he was remarkably good at translating Trevor's feelings into technical musical language for Stephen.

Stephen is a master of pastiche, with an extraordinary ability to create a sound that seems to echo something you've heard before but eludes identification. Everything he produced fitted in harmoniously with what we had rehearsed and was appropriate to mood and theme. It was stirring and moving in the way that had been asked. Most of all I admired some of the music later in the production concerning the build-up to Ralph's death. In that piece Stephen moved subtly away from nineteenth-century pastiche into a more modern, although unobtrusive sound. That reinforced my belief that it is less necessary than it might seem to adhere to period style in such work. Stephen is a brilliant composer who is capable of reflecting appropriate mood and feelings within his own style. Trevor would disagree, but I believe we could have allowed much more scope for a less conventional, twentieth-century score blended with the necessary period pieces; I do not believe it would have intruded on the spirit of the production. Stephen's only regret was that we would not be exploring in depth musical techniques of combining words and music. In dramatic terms there would not be much room for experimenting with techniques.

As the set was moved into the Aldwych Theatre at the beginning of June, we decided to attempt a first full run of the first play at Floral Street. Also, for the first time, we would try and add the music cues.

After the week of work at the Rainbow Theatre we needed a very different type of work. All those days were focused on technical and mechanical problems. Before moving into the final phase of full technical and dress rehearsals we needed desperately to remember where it had all begun: a company of actors telling a story. So, trying hard to forget all practical and physical considerations the company went right through the first play, sitting once again in a circle. Trevor stressed the need to remember to share the story and pass on the baton. We sat in the bare room at Floral Street; all the furniture had been transferred to the Aldwych. The exhausted company told the story with a regained calmness, gentleness and respect for each other. The story shone through as the actors invested great love in the work and each other.

On Sunday 1 June the company, still shattered, agreed to come in and spend a day sorting out costume problems. For the first time all the costumes for Play One were gathered together at Floral Street. Rows and rows of carefully marked Victorian clothes greeted our eyes as we walked in to rehearsal. Slowly, we spent the day working through the play, scene by scene, solely to calculate costume changes. Although exhausting, we finished the day elated at what John Napier had created and more aware than ever of the practical complexities that would be ahead.

We began the technical rehearsal on Monday 2 June at the Aldwych Theatre, knowing we had three days to finish the technical work as in any normal production. The dress rehearsal also had to be done before the first public preview performance on Thursday 5th. To design the lighting we had brought in David Hersey, who had one afternoon's meeting beforehand and had seen the run of Play One. Through watching the show he had prepared nearly all of it on his own. Some lighting designers work out rough, approximate lighting states for each scene before the technical rehearsal with the actors begins. David Hersey appears to do everything on the spot, with the actors. His precise and careful lighting schemes leave no room for guesswork. Using a large number of "beam lights", stage lights with a fine, pencil-thin beam adapted for use as moving spotlights, he began lighting the show. These lights allowed the possibility of picking out individual faces in a crowd, or specific objects on the set without much light spilling elsewhere. David had suggested using this technique some weeks earlier, and now we saw the impressive results of the system as he organised subtly moving light focuses around the rapidly changing shapes and configurations on the stage. This procedure of painting with lights could only be done after David had spent hours with very careful focusing on his carefully designed rig. The work was helped by the excellent relationship between John Napier and David Hersey from their previous work together. This process, in addition to the huge task of the general lighting of John Napier's set, was precise and slow. Jane Tamlyn patiently sat next to him for many hours with headphones on, translating David's instructions to the lighting crew.

Costume changes and furniture movement, in spite of the work at the Rainbow, also took much longer than we had imagined. Also, as the production was so much under-rehearsed, Trevor insisted on acting work going on at the same time as the technical work. Many directors prefer to separate the final points of the acting process from the technical preparation, but not Trevor. Much to the frustration of many actors, he continually stopped the technicals to work on acting and directing problems. He reasoned that with everything in such a chaotic state it was crucial to have a thorough technical rehearsal however long it took. Similarly, for safety's sake each truck movement had to be painstakingly worked through again and again until everyone on stage was aware of their exact position in relation to the trucks. Then, we had our first accident. In spite of all the elaborate precautions we had become a little more relaxed in our use of the trucks. John Napier was still concerned about the safety of the lower one, and the support rope was released for a moment to demonstrate how a safety winch might be attached. At that moment a man fell over and lost hold of the rope and the truck began rolling downstage towards John Woodvine. He saw it coming and leapt off on to the floor between the stalls seats and the stage. Realising it was not going to stop he lay flat as it came off the edge of the stage into the second row of seats. It also just missed Trevor and Susan Littler who jumped off the gangway that thrust out from the stage through the seats. In the dark, it was difficult to see what was going on and we realised how John's instinct to lie down had probably saved his life. Now, extra safety measures were incorporated into the set, including, in addition to a massive winch, scaffolding poles jut-

John Woodvine and Roger Rees

Trevor Nunn explaining the opening to the second play on set at the Rainbow Theatre

ting out through the stage and set in concrete underneath, to act as a fail-safe stop system if the trucks should ever run away again.

The remaining lighting, costumes, props and related technical troubles were only part of the story. The music cues had been only estimated before we transferred to the Aldwych Theatre. The runthrough at Floral Street had been the only opportunity to try them out. We were now discovering many necessary modifications. On occasions we even needed new cues to be written. Stephen Oliver ran backwards and forwards throughout the technical rehearsal orchestrating new cues to order. These were transcribed and given to the band to sight-read and play on the spot.

Many company narrative sections had not yet been rehearsed or in some cases even allocated to the actors. John Caird sat calculating who could deliver which lines and I hastily passed on the new script to each member of the company, trying to explain what would be happening on the stage whilst this was being spoken. Some of the company were confused to the point of near-hysteria. They already had enough problems working out character changes and entrances and exits as well as which furniture they had to set and strike without having to cope with more script. Many were not even sure of the sequence of scenes which had been altered several times in the few weeks before. In addition, David Edgar was doing on the spot rewrites which he passed to his diligent script assistant Sarah Spare to copy out and bring back to the company.

This process continued throughout Monday and Tuesday. By Wednesday morning we were only just past halfway through the play, with many of the most difficult scenes still ahead. By Wednesday afternoon we were in despair. With no chance of even finishing the technical work by Thursday afternoon we had completely gone off schedule.

The directors and Simon Opie had an emergency meeting and Trevor phoned David Brierley, RSC general manager. We decided to cancel the first preview. Though nearly all the tickets had been sold in advance, we had no choice. The show could not possibly open in its present state, vastly under-rehearsed and technically still dangerous. The Royal Shakespeare Company would of course lose that night's revenue, but it had to be done. The box office staff would have a long night and next day ahead trying to contact as many of the public as possible who had bought tickets. What was even worse was that we had as yet no way of even guaranteeing the second public performance. We still had a long way to go before the dress rehearsal. We were also very conscious of the potential devastating effect the cancellation would have on the acting company's morale. An already exhausted company now were to be told that the agonising technical work would be continued without the audience they both craved and feared.

On Thursday morning Trevor broke the news to the company. Disheartened and partly relieved, but not defeated, they all agreed to push everything at high speed to enable us to dress rehearse by the evening. After hours of gruelling work the promised dress rehearsal could not be achieved—we were still not at the end of the play by the late evening. We planned the dress rehearsal for the following afternoon just before the first public performance. At another midnight meeting the directors agreed not to cancel the second performance, although we still feared opening without a full dress rehearsal. We all felt the growing excitement that was present in the company.

After more hours of technical work on Friday morning we finally managed to begin a dress rehearsal. As well as everything else ever since the beginning of the project it ran over time and had to stop before the end. By the time the actors reached the point of their short break before the performance we had still not dress rehearsed the entire *Romeo and Juliet* sequence and ending of the play. We agreed to go ahead come what may.

At seven o'clock on Friday 6 June the audience began to arrive as the shattered and exhilarated company began to prepare for their first contact with an audience. After nearly eight months of work behind closed doors none of us really had any perspective left on what we had created.

Trevor Nunn gives notes at the Rainbow Theatre

FIRST NIGHT AND THE CRITICS

We were not sure how to go about informing the public that they were about to see what was really no more than a dress rehearsal. We were agreed on a short announcement just before the beginning of the production, when another idea was suggested. As part of Trevor's concept of direct physical contact from the set to the audience, he also asked the company to go out in costume and greet the audience and talk with them before the performance and during the intervals. The idea was to create from the onset a feeling of association between actors and audience by inviting the public to become a part of all that would take place. With the band playing themes from the show on stage, the acting company were to mingle with the public arriving in the auditorium and strike up conversations, not in character but simply as themselves. They were to tell the audience about the rehearsal situation themselves, and could explain that in its present state the performance was likely to be very long.

And so it was. It lasted over four and a half hours, finishing near midnight. But, to our amazement, only a tiny trickle of people left before the end, and those who remained applauded vigorously and left the theatre in a high state of excitement. From the beginning of the performance to the end they seemed to be captivated by the story—rarely distracted and rarely lacking in concentration. Trevor, John, David and I were relieved and pleased, and the company were delighted. Although, naturally, an insecure performance, the company had against the odds managed a compelling one. Trevor's slow technical process had paid off and although under-rehearsed the adrenalin had flowed and the extraordinary spirit of the company ensemble had helped them through.

In analysis later that night and into the early hours the directors and David knew that it was good but that it had a long way to go. The adrenalin of the first preview had to be replaced by a stronger technical confidence. But much more than that, it needed to be made shorter and tighter. We had argued many times about cutting the text of both plays but had always found it hard actually to achieve. There was invariably one of the four of us who wanted to defend a particular moment or sometimes even a single line of the script. The actors had pleaded for cuts, but as Trevor remarked, everyone was keen to propose other actors' and actresses' scenes and lines as targets for cutting but not their own. In fact, one or two members of the company did offer their own lines, but on the whole Trevor was right. In our private meetings Trevor was particularly defensive against proposed cuts and protective of actors' lines. Surprisingly, David Edgar was normally quick to offer cuts in his own script. But Trevor felt that the morale of individual actors was more important than the overall length and that the work as a whole would suffer if we began to pull back from the attempt at an entire novel as we had always agreed. Much of the experience of watching the production was, he argued, connected intrinsically to the wealth, richness and in fact size of the work. To cut it jeopardised this very quality.

However, some cuts were agreed and prepared for the next afternoon. These alterations were announced to a nervous cast poised with pencils over their beloved scenes. They all knew that the cuts were necessary but some were upset that they had been left so late and others fought hard to protect their character. We tried hard to keep insisting that they were practical cuts that had nothing to do with acting quality. With only a short time before the break before the performance, cuts were rapidly rehearsed. In addition, Trevor implored everyone to trust the story more and to stop holding on to each moment. Pass the baton, trust that the audience are already with or ahead of you. Trevor was sure that fifteen minutes could be taken off with dexterity and speed and a further fifteen minutes with the cuts. Our target had always been about four hours for the first play.

The second preview was an immensely improved piece of work. Increased energy and determination to tell the story quickly gave the performance a shot in the arm. The atmosphere in the house was electric. The slightly shortened length focused concentration in the company and audience. But at the end the audience was ecstatic. They stood for a long standing ovation and the actors had to return again and again to the stage for curtain calls. Now, I felt that we were on the brink of something that was to fulfil Trevor's dreams. The first play worked. The audience would come back for more.

The length had been just over four hours. A few more small cuts were agreed. The last afternoon, before moving on to Play Two, some quick rehearsals took place after a long notes session. Only general notes were given publicly, the detailed personal notes were passed on directly by Trevor, John and myself to the actors as they changed and prepared for each performance. The final of the three performances took place and again the audience rose to their feet and the company left the theatre elated. But Trevor, John, David and I were now even more aware of how hard it would be to put on Play Two. It would be a disastrous anti-climax if the second play faded and failed after the tumultuous reception of the first. We still suspected that it was overwhelmingly long. By our still rough calculations it could easily last six hours. By the end all of the audience might well be in bed at home. The third performance of Play One took place on Saturday 7 June. The first performance of Play Two would take place on Thursday 11 June. We had already cancelled the first preview, originally scheduled for the Wednesday, after cancelling the first preview of Play One. We already knew that even with one extra day we stood little chance of being at all prepared for the public.

We were also aware that for the first play we had at least had the experience of the Rainbow Theatre; now we had to go through a technical rehearsal for a six-hour play completely for the first time, and many of the scenes had only been scarcely rehearsed beforehand. The only factors in our favour were a company propelled on by a great belief in their work, activated by the growing success with the first play. Also, we hoped that this production of the second play would be technically simpler than the first. Learning from our first early experience at the Rainbow there was much less truck movement envisaged in this production and some time would be saved. But we had no illusion about the task ahead.

By the Wednesday night, originally scheduled as the first performance and now as dress rehearsal, we were still not at the end of the technical rehearsal. Although we were working at a much faster pace than we had on the first play, progress was still slow.

Stephen Oliver was now writing and orchestrating new cues all the time. David was cutting and modifying speeches throughout, to be quickly typed by Script Assistant Sarah Spare, John was still allocating narrative speeches to the company for the first time, and I was trying to keep everyone calm and sane. We had discovered in the last few weeks of work on the second play that frequent narrative sections were a strong way of binding together the complex story lines. In our need to reduce its length the narrative passages became more and more important as a means of continuity and introduction between scenes. However, time had run out before these joining sequences could all be rehearsed, although John had begun the process in a gruelling afternoon's work some days before. Now, during the technical rehearsal, more were added. By now the company were surprised at nothing and philosophically accepted without a murmur new lines of script that were handed to them at this late point in time, although they already barely knew whether they were coming or going.

We had to decide either to continue the technical rehearsal on Thursday morning and afternoon, or to cancel another preview, which would have destroyed morale completely. We simply forged ahead the next day and just finished the technical work by the end of the afternoon.

One complex whole section of the play, the events leading to the death of Ralph Nickleby, had only ever been rehearsed for a few hours. In his first draft of the section David had experimented with a new form of narrative technique, with a single *alter ego* Ralph, played by one member of the company. This was to be a way of allowing a form of soliloquy to reflect the inner psychological turmoil in Ralph's mind, expressed in such detail and length by Dickens. It had not seemed to work, however, and we had replaced that single voice with a large group. They were to be present throughout Ralph's last desperate run around London, watching him and, in fact, themselves becoming the physical manifestation of all that was happening around him— the black cloud that he felt following him, the doors that refused him admission, and the walls that enclosed him. But, due to the need for so many of the company before the scene could be rehearsed, it had not been possible to work at it until the last few days of rehearsal. In just a few hours of work John Caird had imaginatively choreographed the entire sequence. He was partly drawing on memories of the exercise of the same scene in the first days at Stratford, but took the ideas much further into a long, carefully organised sequence of mimetic movement and patterns

Ralph Nickleby on his final nightmare journey through London speaks to Mrs Snawley

all over the stage, which represented a major breakthrough with that part of the play. During the technical rehearsal, David Hersey had to try and follow the ever-moving sea of bodies with lights, whilst creating in light different atmospheric reflections of the internal movement of mood and tone.

The sequence culminates in the death of Ralph as he hangs himself in the lonely attic of his home where his dead son Smike once used to sleep. John Napier had suggested a solution to the staging problems of the hanging that now needed trying for the first time. Ralph would prepare to hang himself realistically with a rope, but at the last moment we would move into a symbolic, though still dramatic, presentation of the moment of death. Ralph would climb on a chair, beneath the imaginary black hook in the ceiling, and jerk the rope around his neck upward. At the same instant a weighted dummy on a rope would be dropped from the lighting bridge over the front top of the proscenium arch into the trapdoor opening immediately below. This would be synchronised with a violent lighting change and music cue.

The first time the dummy was dropped it missed the trapdoor opening. The second time it seemed to come down in slow motion, caught up on the way. The third attempt almost worked. We had no more time for experiment. We dreaded what might happen at the performance itself.

Although the technical rehearsal was complete, this time there had been no dress rehearsal at all. The company once again went out to mingle with the audience, this time warning them that the performance might be six hours long.

It was a remarkable performance, although five-and-a-half hours in length. Few people left, even though public transport had ended some time before the end, and the response by the audience was overwhelming. In many ways I felt that potentially the second play was indeed the more interesting of the two. However, five and a half hours was much too long and we knew that although the audience had been loyal and enthusiastic to the end they were under severe strain. In particular, the final section was difficult for an audience to stay with. The structure of the play allowed two intervals. The problem of the new plots and characters being introduced near the end, Madeline Bray, Arthur Gride, Walter Bray, Peg Sliderskew, was intensified by a second interval which came when most people would normally have expected to be on their way home. We tried to find a way of taking out the second interval but could not without major rewriting and restructuring. It was too late for that now.

For the second and final performance of the second play before Saturday, when both parts were to be put together for the first time, more cuts were made—this time more severe and painful for those affected. Again, speed and greater dexterity were asked of the company. Even more than Play One it needed to move at a breathtaking pace. Trevor rehearsed a totally new first scene to the second play, and the company enthusiastically helped.

Over half an hour came off the performance, so that we were at least now within the conceivable range of our target of four and a half hours for that second play. The audience responded enthusiastically and at length at the end, but still seemed weary.

On Saturday 14 June, the following day, the plays were put together for the first time. We didn't even know as yet whether it would be possible to change over from the end of Play One to prepare for Play Two, given the short break between performances. With Play One beginning at two o'clock and ending just after six o'clock, and Play Two opening at seven o'clock, time was tight. We also feared that the strain on the company would tell in the length of the second play which was still due to end around midnight.

Having gained confidence from the first few performances the company had eagerly looked forward to this day. Somehow the work was never quite satisfying in the two separate halves. Some actors and actresses felt incomplete after an evening performance of just Part One. Although exhausted from the week's strenuous work, the opportunity to put it all together at last, after many months of work, triggered what little energy was left. The performance was by far the best so far and the obviously approving audience response encouraged further advances. At the end of the evening the most extraordinary experience took place as the audience stood and shouted and cried out for the company to come again and again for multiple curtain calls. Even with the house lights full up they refused to let the actors go as they applauded and called "Bravo!". The curtain call alone added fifteen minutes to the performance time. Roger Rees, leading the call, even brought on the band and stage management for calls and finally the exhausted cast clapped the audience themselves and left the stage.

None of us had ever experienced such a reception in our entire lives. Even Trevor had never had such an ovation for one of his works before. Someone could only recall the first night of Peter Brook's *Midsummer Night's Dream* at Stratford as a comparison. The company were elated and some tearful, genuinely moved at the audience's response. Clearly, something very special was taking place between actors and audience from their first meeting before the show to the curtain call at the end. The audience were sharing the process of storytelling and felt that at the end of the marathon day's performance they too had been involved. They were in some way applauding themselves.

Amidst all the growing excitement, there was one great disappointment. The houses were not full throughout all the first performances and advance bookings were very poor. *The Greeks*, John Barton's three-part epic adaptation of various Greek tragedies, had recently almost completely sold out just on advance booking. We had hoped to do at least half as well. There didn't seem to have been much advance publicity and the actors were frustrated at achieving such an audience response with rows of empty seats before them. We just had to wait for the reviews and word of mouth to pick up sales.

The major press day was scheduled for the following Saturday, matinee and evening, although some critics preferred to see it on the Monday and Tuesday after. Before then there were three more performances of Play One and only two of Play Two.

During each day specific scenes were rehearsed, notes given and further minor cuts implemented. Each performance grew in confidence and the standing ovations continued, although not always quite at the pitch of the first Saturday, and now half the seats were empty. Even on the press day itself, Saturday 21 June, many seats were still not filled.

The press performance was, like the previous Saturday's, a triumph. Once again there was a long and ecstatic standing ovation at the end of the evening. Whatever the critics said, the public were expressing their response unambiguously. By now the length of performance of the two plays was close to four and four and a half hours, as originally hoped, although many of the company were still unhappy with the length, especially of the second play. But Trevor, in his belief in the work in its present state and length, resisted further cuts.

The reviews were published as the week went on. Although many were favourable, many were negative or at least mixed. I was stunned by the disparity between the overall critical response and that given by the public.

John Barber in *The Daily Telegraph* of 23 June, said: "But the adaptation runs on so long that the persistent sermonising becomes tedious, and the coincidence in the yarn (it's hardly a plot) becomes laughable. . . . Acting opportunities for the principals prove unrewarding, thanks to the fatal flatness of Dickens' characters." Although he admires the ambition of it all he concludes: "Lovers of the novelist will revel in it. Those who are not will be wise to keep away".

Although liking above all David Threlfall's Smike and a few other performances Benedict Nightingale, *New Statesman*, 27 June, said: "But the evening might still have profited from a going-over with both visual and verbal secateurs. If the proper critical test is dramatic effectiveness, and not strict fidelity to Dickens, there can be no strong case for retaining, say, the Kenwigs sub-plot. If fidelity is the criterion, and we're to see the play as an entertaining crib or potted classic in 3-D, why are a couple of sentences elaborated (and, incidentally, distorted) into a long parody of early nineteenth-century Shakespeare, with Romeo and Juliet given last minute Lazarus treatment and the revived Paris married off to a female Benvolio". He, like John Barber, felt it all too long and also felt it to be: "too festive and lacking in bite . . . it is easier to imagine a tougher, harsher, angrier production, one that ventured more often and whole-heartedly into the ugly grotesque . . .".

Felix Barber, *Evening News*, 23 June, liked the second play more but wrote of the first: "*The Life and Adventures of Nicholas Nickleby,* his widowed mother and doleful sister Kate, were enacted in a succession of short scenes. Some were pointless, others verged on the incomprehensible and nearly all were devoid of dramatic tension. Ruthless pruning to three hours and a single performance would not be a sacrilege but a salvation".

Francis King, *The Sunday Telegraph*, 29 June, disliked the length and completeness of it all: ". . . Mr Edgar has decided to give us both the best and worst of him in full".

Peter Jenkins, *Spectator*, 28 June, also found it too long and believed the novel to be quite unsuitable for stage adaptation: "The Dotheboys scenes lend themselves perfectly to the theatre and are well done; they provide the only moment in the whole of the two evenings which is seriously upsetting rather than sentimentally moving. The remainder of the first evening is theatrically a disaster. The Mantalini episodes are tiresomely un-funny—Kate Nickleby is such a pill, the Kenwigs/Lillyvick sub-plot (of which there is more to come in Part Two) is lacking in all theatrical potential and the Crummles episodes although one of the most admired parts of the book, become too much of a self-regarding theatrical cliché when re-imported from the novel to the stage".

Milton Shulman, *Evening Standard*, 26 June, felt that it just "isn't very good theatre". However, Trevor noticed that due to the ecstatic standing ovation he was stuck in the Dress Circle and had difficulty in leaving. A woman next to him was in tears. How, Trevor wondered later, was it possible for him to consider the whole project a failure?

Perhaps the strongest criticism of all came from Michael Billington in the *Guardian*, whose review was captioned: "A Triumph of Perversity". Although believing it to be "very fine", he could not help wondering "if the whole thing wasn't a waste of the RSC's amazing resources". He believed the overall result to be "less drama than acted narrative". He commends many individual performances but concludes with the question: ". . . should it have been done at all?".

Finally, Colin Chambers, *Morning Star*, 26 June, like Benedict Nightingale preferred the Shared Experience version of *Bleak House* that had been performed "without costume and props and with only five actors in a version that was tighter than the RSC's, as gripping and more relevant".

Robert Cushman in *The Observer* of 29 June spearheaded the defence in a direct answer to some of the negative reviews: "The critical reaction has astonished me: hours of pleasure, acknowledged as such, and people start wondering whether it should have been done." Although he found the Dotheboys Hall scenes lacking in horror and humour and some of the performances not fully enough developed, he lists numerous excellent performances and says at the beginning of the review that "There is a lot to be said for length".

James Fenton in *The Sunday Times* of 29 June, praised at length Roger Rees and David Threlfall among others, but in particular admired the hugeness and variety of it all. Seeing it almost like a long opera in which many different turns and changes are possible, he concluded it to be: "a marvellous show and a very valuable experiment".

John Elsom, *The Listener*, 26 June, analysed and admired the work as a whole, and in particular, a long list of performances and the adaptation itself: "Edgar's journalistic streak and his love of shock-horror-probe, makes him an excellent adaptor of Dickens, and Trevor Nunn, who directed with John Caird, has put the full range of his excellent company on display".

The *Daily Express* critic, 28 June, summed it up as: ". . . a monumental experience which spread over two evenings and lasting more than eight hours employs forty-three actors playing around a hundred and fifty roles. Every one a gem".

Barry Baker in the *Daily Mail*, 23 June, also praised the production and admired the way it "preserved the astonishing qualities of *Nicholas Nickleby*—with compassion, and the humorous exposure of the absurd pretensions of early Victorian society".

Lynne Truss, *The Times Educational Supplement*, 23–27 June, had her review entitled: "Dickens would cheer". After praising many individual performances she concluded: "By adapting this novel the RSC has done Dickens great service but the honour is reciprocated by the opportunity he has given them to explore their own methods of theatricality".

Although Sheridan Morley, *Punch*, 2 July, thought that ninety minutes could be "shaved off its overall running time", it was still a fine piece of work. "If the question is do we actually need a stage *Nickleby*, the answer must, I believe, be yes; if the question is do we need one at quite this length, the answer gets a bit more uncertain."

B. A. Young, *Financial Times*, enthuses about many individual performances and describes the whole day's performance as a "long Saturday of extreme pleasure". He also admired the complexity and variety of it all. "Evidently the direction, by two directors and an assistant, is endlessly inventive. . . . The whole thing is a triumph and if this is the kind of thing the company devises to save money (as they say it is), may they long remain in similar difficulties."

John Walker, *Now!* magazine, 4–10 July, concludes it to be "popular theatre at its finest . . . a feast of a play that will provide sustenance for any audience. It manages to put a whole society on stage—and one that in its divisions of class and interest is not far removed from our own—to create a wild and pulsing panorama full of detailed particularity, that makes most of what is on the London stage seem narrow and unnecessarily confined".

J. C. Trewin wrote about the overall success of the venture in the unity that it provides and the diversity that it exhibits: "Somehow the RSC has managed to unify the book for the stage in a rightly stick-at-nothing version by David Edgar . . . I have never known a more elaborate theatrical treatment of any novel. . . . What the audience get is a splendid phantasmagoria, scene dissolving rapidly into scene, everyone in the RSC mobilised to keep the narrative moving . . .".

Ned Chaillet, *The Times*, 23 June, picks out many of the actors for praise and then concludes that "the present RSC is a national treasure".

On the whole the score was about even. We were all bitterly disappointed with the notices and I was astounded that not one had mentioned the euphoric way that the audience responded at the end of the performance. Few, if any, of the reviews were ecstatic and many were distinctly negative. Only one or two had seriously attempted to analyse what the production had achieved, or tried to achieve. Perhaps the most devastating of all were those who asked why we had bothered at all.

But the public response was quite different. From the first previews onwards letters flooded into the theatre—to the directors, members of the company, even one to the stage management. Many poured out thanks for the pleasure they had received and some even claimed that the production had moved them deeply and changed their lives in some way. By the end of the six-week run we had a noticeboard crammed from top to bottom with letters of praise from the audience, more than the RSC could ever remember having seen.

Yet, largely due to the mixed critical reception, a large number of seats remained empty. The audience was saying it was the greatest theatrical experience they had ever had, the press was lukewarm. Deterred by the length and the cost of two productions many people stayed away. By the end of the first week the numbers of the audience were just beginning to pick up. It seemed that the word of mouth was gradually becoming stronger than the notices in the press. Then, on 8 July, things changed rapidly.

Bernard Levin published an article in *The Times* that analysed the intention behind the production in fine detail and attacked the critics for not praising it themselves. At length he reported in extravagant and rich terms of admiration his feelings about the production: "some of the critical comment that has greeted the production makes one despair not just of criticism but of the human race. . . . The response has exhibited that most dreadful of all the *vices anglais*, the terror of being thought enthusiastic; most of the reviewers have spent their time carefully balancing praise for one detail against regret for another. . . . There is only one way to behave at the Aldwych; to surrender completely to the truth, which is that not for many years has London's theatre seen anything so richly joyous, so immoderately rife with pleasure, drama, colour and entertainment, so life-enhancing, yea-saying and fecund, so—in the one word which embraces all these and more—so Dickensian. . . . It is a celebration of love and justice that is true to the spirit of Dickens' belief that those are the fulcrums on which the universe is moved, and the consequence is that we come out not merely delighted but strengthened, not just entertained but uplifted, not only affected but changed".

From the next morning onward the box office was flooded with ticket requests. The production sold out for the rest of its short six-week run.

The Crummles Theatre Company sing "England, Arise"

Roger Rees at the Rainbow Theatre

AFTERMATH

By the end of the run there were more letters from the public than any of us had ever seen before about a single production. One after another people wrote to us saying how they were enthralled and moved by what they had seen and, in Levin's words, how they had come out "uplifted and changed".

The greatest problem was that there were now no more seats available and hundreds of people were phoning and writing daily for tickets. One journalist, Frank Giles, Deputy Editor of *The Sunday Times*, 20 July, even published an article six days before the end of the run asking how we could dare to let it end so soon: "When is a theatrical performance a masterpiece? One answer is when it is the current Royal Shakespeare Company's production of *Nicholas Nickleby* at the Aldwych Theatre.... Of all the remarkable aspects of these remarkable performances, perhaps the most outstanding is that they are due to end at the Aldwych on 26 July. No revival is planned. This seems incredible. It is as though someone with a perfectly new Rolls-Royce decided to junk it".

In response to the public's pressure Trevor began to explore the possibilities of a further life for the production. However, the run could not simply be extended, as we had already planned, announced and sold tickets for the next few months of performances of the Royal Shakespeare Company. The other productions had already been organised and contracts had been signed.

The second possibility was to transfer *Nicholas Nickleby* to another theatre and run as a commercial operation. But calculations showed that to be a financial impossibility. With such a large cast and complex set it would need a minimum long run of many months to recuperate enough financial return to make it worthwhile. We knew that the company would not want to stay with just one piece of work for so long. In many cases of transfer many actors could be replaced over a long run, but due to the nature of rehearsal and the carefully created company attitude, this would soon lead to an inferior production.

The only possibility was to bring back *Nicholas Nickleby* near the end of the year for a second short run at the Aldwych Theatre. However, to achieve this, we knew we had to have the agreement of the vast majority of the company. Although it would not be convenient for many, the belief in the work, the continual excitement and ecstatic response of the audiences convinced them to agree. After weeks of negotiations in which we realised that we would have to lose a few of the company we were able to plan the second run of *Nicholas Nickleby*. We had to replace Ben Kingsley who had a wonderful career-changing offer to play Gandhi in a major new film. Juliet Hammond-Hill, Graham Crowden and Susan Littler also had to leave the project. In addition to finding a new Squeers, Mr Crummles, Madeline Bray and Kate, we had also to replace one or two others.

The second run continued the snowball effect of the first. In spite of a relatively short re-rehearsal period the production was quickly back to its full strength. Although there had been continual requests by many of the company to shorten the production, the length was not greatly altered although a few minor cuts were made. Indeed, one scene that had never been greatly successful was rewritten in a slightly longer form. The major attempt at shortening the second play was, alas, not successful. We tried to take out the second interval during the second play, because of a feeling that the audience would probably rather not have to take a break at such a late point in the evening if instead it could finish fifteen minutes earlier. Also, the concentration on the Gride/Bray plot was never as focused as it should be at that late point in the evening. To achieve this a restructuring of the play had to take place and scenes played in a different order. After several days of work it was tried before an audience, but we finally had to reject the new plans. In fact, the performance was only a little shorter and felt longer. The interval was reinstated, although the new order of scenes was mainly kept intact, and I felt that the production had gained in strength from this process of change.

The only major trauma during the dress rehearsals and technical preparation was the unexpected premature birth of Trevor's and Janet's first child. Halfway through the technical rehearsals he had to rush off to the hospital. A few days later all was well and the company were relieved to hear about the healthy state of Joshua Nunn.

This time, the critical response was much more positive. One review after another enthused about the production. It seemed that for once much of the most enthusiastic critical reception had been preceded by an overwhelming public reaction. The newcomers to the production, Fulton MacKay as Squeers, Harriet Walter as Madeline Bray, Emily Richard, who had rejoined us to play Kate, and Christopher Benjamin as Mr Crummles, all received praise.

As the weeks went by, the flood of letters from the public continued. In addition there was also now a pile of letters from various organisations and managements enquiring about the possibilities of transfers, tours, and films. From countries as far apart as Australia and the United States came proposals for *Nicholas Nickleby* to visit. A number of different television and film groups suggested that *Nicholas Nickleby* should be filmed. Most of the film suggestions proposed a highly cut two or three-hour version that would be filmed at the theatre with a live audience. Trevor firmly dismissed all such offers. He said that if it were ever to be filmed it must be in its entirety and it would have to be redirected specifically for the cameras. In other words, it would have to be a full studio made version that would take many weeks and cost a vast amount to make. Otherwise, it would only be a shadow of what the audience had experienced and would be an inaccurate and unrepresentative record for posterity. Similarly, any transfer to Broadway would have to be of the entire work. Trevor was not prepared to take a specially cut version. It must be all or nothing. The calculations proved it to be virtually impossible, even if the Equity problems concerning British actors working in the USA could be solved. The show would have to make a considerable loss however successful it was, and the initial cost would be very high—higher than anything the RSC had ever contemplated before. None of the suggested propositions seemed possible, but negotiations continued nonetheless.

Once again the actors became very tired, and understudies went on. In a remarkable gesture of company goodwill the entire cast had agreed to understudy each other. Even Roger

Rees, John Woodvine and the other leading actors had agreed to understudy at least one role. Although it took me a week to work out, I found a way of covering every single possible understudy situation. If one actor or actress was off, their different roles and lines might be covered by three or perhaps four different members of the company. Only two actors from outside were needed, Sally Nesbitt and Hilary Townley, to cover some of the female roles.

The actor we became increasingly worried about was David Threlfall, although he never actually had to miss a performance. During the second run he became gradually weaker and had various symptoms of illness, though the doctors could not find anything specifically wrong. Somehow, as a result of his total involvement in the character, David seemed to have been affected by the role of Smike. The sickly, dying Smike left his mark on David between performances as well as during them. He only just seemed to make it to the end of the run—then he took a long needed rest. Only looking back many months later did he come to understand how much Smike had affected his own life.

The entire run had sold out once again, and we received many letters expressing disappointment from people who could not get tickets. We knew that in spite of continued enthusiasm some of the company would not want to bring back *Nicholas Nickleby* for just another run at the Aldwych Theatre—they were keen to move on to other work. We had all lived with *Nicholas Nickleby* for well over a year. The only hope for a further life was through the American possibilities and the television proposals.

One television proposal had stood out from the other. Prime Time Television, an independent company capable of making programmes for transmission on the new Channel Four, had been willing to contemplate a nine-part television version based on Trevor's guidelines—the complete production properly prepared for television. It now seemed as though they might be able to raise enough money from the USA and from other sources. Similarly, one of the producers interested in taking *Nicholas Nickleby* to New York seemed to have made progress against almost impossible odds and had raised a large amount of money towards the project. But even by the end of the second run nothing could be guaranteed.

At a company meeting these facts were explained to the company. Trevor proposed a third and final run at the Aldwych Theatre beginning near the end of April, ending on 20 June. Then, if all went well with negotiations, after a short two or three week break *Nicholas Nickleby* would be filmed throughout the summer. Finally, if the impossible could be achieved, *Nicholas Nickleby* would go to New York for a season until the end of the year. However, even though they had to commit themselves to a further run at the Aldwych the other two projects could not yet be promised.

Once again, asked to give everything and risk the possibility of little in return, that extraordinary company agreed to the plan. Only a few felt unable to take part.

Whilst talks with the USA and Prime Time Television continued, the third run was planned. In agreement with the acting company's request that only six performances a week instead of the usual eight should be undertaken, another production was conceived using the same basic set, as it was not possible to put it up and take it down every few days. Some members of the *Nicholas Nickleby* company were also involved in that production of *The Knight of the Burning Pestle*, and others were in a new play, *The Accrington Pals*, at the second RSC theatre in London, The Warehouse.

The major casualties were once again Madeline Bray and Squeers. Tim Spall also withdrew from the project and Ian McNeice, having sorted out his personal problems from back in Stratford, rejoined the company to take over Tim's parts. Lucy Gutteridge came in as Madeline Bray and Alun Armstrong joined us to play Squeers. Hilary Townley, the understudy, moved into the production as Julie Peasgood, now pregnant, had to leave.

This time the entire allocation of tickets sold out ten days before the production even opened. During the second run, *Nicholas Nickleby* had gathered an extraordinary list of acting, directing, writing and design awards from every major theatre award panel. At the Society of West End Theatre awards alone *Nicholas Nickleby* had been given five awards. Perhaps the greatest irony was the Best Direction award, given by the theatre critics, many of whom had written negative reviews. The popularity of the show had grown steadily over the months and the public had waited with eagerness for the third run.

Again the audience response was tumultuous and the replacement performances excellent. Personally, I felt that all was not quite as well as before. The somewhat rushed rehearsal period caused some problems although the show did settle down after a few days. But it seemed to me that there had been a shift in the relationship between the company and the audience. Now, the public were coming expecting to see an extraordinary piece of work. They had already heard so much about it. Similarly, the company knew when to expect certain audience responses and how to achieve them. Already, I believe, we had to deal with the problems of a show that had been in existence for some time. Actors and directors worked hard at trying to identify and combat any negative changes and were often successful. The level of energy and concentration necessary to keep the production at its highest point of achievement was enormous and could not always be there. Nevertheless the final run was another triumphant success; the audience, at least, did not detect a difference.

Halfway through the run the television film was confirmed to a delighted company. At the same time as the confirmation was going through, it was announced in the press that the Old Vic company, due to Arts Council withdrawal of funds, had ceased to operate. The television company proposed that the Old Vic would be a wonderful place to film the production of *Nicholas Nickleby*. At this moment of writing that plan has been agreed and filming is about to begin.

The American offer has been agreed and the production will open at the Plymouth Theatre in October 1981. However, the actors are resisting the idea of eight performances a week for fourteen weeks—even if it is Broadway. It is only the actors who really experience and understand the full emotional and physical strain of such a work as *Nicholas Nickleby*.

How can you successfully transfer from stage to film a live theatre performance of such length and complexity as *Nicholas Nickleby*? How can you create on television the all-important relationship between actor and audience? How will *Nicholas Nickleby* be received by an American audience not so close to our own Dickensian inheritance? These questions will be approached in the coming months and will be another story in themselves.

As I reread once again what I've written about the *Nicholas Nickleby* story I feel that it is a very personal view of the work. I know Trevor, John, David, Roger or any of the others in the project would see it in very different ways. It is so big, so rich, so diverse in its achievements that it is open to many points of view.

Nicholas Nickleby has taught me more about the process of acting, directing and dramatic writing than any other piece of work I know. The production is itself a monument to the tireless and committed company that created it. The questions concerning Dickens and his great humanity have been transposed by the actors themselves into the lives of all who have worked on the project and those who have seen it. It is a rare theatrical achievement and behind it all I believe is the guiding hand of Trevor and his epic conception of what the RSC could achieve at its best. It affects all our work on Shakespeare and the other great dramatists. As Nicholas de Jongh pointed out in his review of the second run of *Nicholas Nickleby*, the production is essentially Shakespearean in its approach and use of space.

The actors' emotional and physical commitment to the work is at the centre of its success. Only with that remarkable ensemble spirit and attitude could *Nicholas Nickleby* have succeeded on such a scale.

As *Nicholas Nickleby* goes on to be filmed and moves to Broadway, I leave the RSC for other work. I, like others who now leave or left the project earlier, need to move on to other plays. But I believe that we will all carry with us the immense knowledge that we have gained from Dickens and the process of the adaptation. I am sure that it will not be the last large-scale adaptation at the RSC or elsewhere. But it is only with subsidy that such work can ever be carried out—a subsidy that allows resources to be exploited in every possible way. *Nicholas Nickleby* is the living proof that theatres must be allowed enough time and enough resources to create great work. *Nicholas Nickleby* could not ever be achieved in a few weeks of rushed rehearsal.

One of the reasons for *Nicholas Nickleby* was a fight against cuts in subsidy. I believe that we have all learnt how much that subsidy is desperately needed if we are to break the circle of under-financed, hasty work and often inferior results. The theatres in this country must have the opportunity to experiment and explore if our live theatre is to survive into the next century.

We never share enough with our public the way we work. We can never assume that our audience will always be there; we must come out and meet them. That is why I believe that the *Nicholas Nickleby* story should be told.

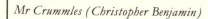
Mr Crummles (Christopher Benjamin)

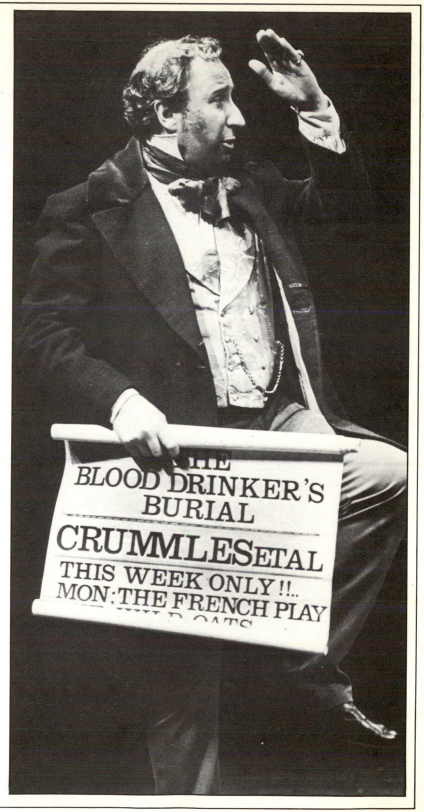

THE NICHOLAS NICKLEBY COMPANY

THE NICKLEBY FAMILY

NICHOLAS NICKLEBY	Roger Rees
KATE NICKLEBY	Susan Littler/Emily Richard
RALPH NICKLEBY	John Woodvine
MRS NICKLEBY	Jane Downs

LONDON

NEWMAN NOGGS	Edward Petherbridge
HANNAH	Clare Travers-Deacon/Hilary Townley
MISS LA CREEVY	Rose Hill
SIR MATTHEW PUPKER	David Lloyd Meredith
MR BONNEY	Terence Harvey/Andrew Hawkins
IRATE GENTLEMAN	Patrick Godfrey
FURIOUS GENTLEMAN	Ben Kingsley
FLUNKEY	Timothy Kightley
MUFFIN BOYS	Alun Armstrong, Lucy Gutteridge, Andrew Hawkins, Ian McNeice, Timothy Spall
MR SNAWLEY	William Maxwell
SNAWLEY MAJOR	Janet Dale
SNAWLEY MINOR	Clare Travers-Deacon/Hilary Townley
BELLING	Stephen Rashbrook
WILLIAM	John McEnery
WAITRESSES	Sharon Bower, Juliet Hammond-Hill, Sally Nesbitt, Harriet Walter
COACHMAN	Clyde Pollitt
MR MANTALINI	John McEnery
MADAME MANTALINI	Thelma Whiteley
FLUNKEY	Griffith Jones
MISS KNAG	Janet Dale
RICH LADIES	Sharon Bower, Shirley King
MILLINERS	Suzanne Bertish, Sharon Bower, Ian East, Lucy Gutteridge, Juliet Hammond-Hill, Cathryn Harrison, William Maxwell, Julie Peasgood, Stephen Rashbrook, Clare Travers-Deacon, Hilary Townley, Harriet Walter

YORKSHIRE

MR SQUEERS	Ben Kingsley/Fulton MacKay/Alun Armstrong
MRS SQUEERS	Lila Kaye
SMIKE	David Threlfall
PHIB	Cathryn Harrison/Sally Nesbitt
FANNY SQUEERS	Suzanne Bertish
YOUNG WACKFORD SQUEERS	Timothy Spall/Ian McNeice
JOHN BROWDIE	Bob Peck
TILDA PRICE	Julie Peasgood/Cathryn Harrison
TOMKINS	William Maxwell
COATES	Andrew Hawkins
GRAYMARSH	Alan Gill
JENNINGS	Terence Harvey
MOBBS	Christopher Ravenscroft
BOLDER	Mark Tandy

PITCHER	Sharon Bower
JACKSON	Nicholas Gecks
COBBEY	John Matshikiza/John McEnery
PETERS	Teddy Kempner
SPROUTER	
ROBERTS	Ian East
MCTAGGART	Neil Phillips

LONDON AGAIN

MR KENWIGS	Patrick Godfrey
MRS KENWIGS	Shirley King
MORLEENA KENWIGS	Clare Travers-Deacon/Hilary Townley
MR LILLYVICK	Timothy Kightley
MISS PETOWKER	Cathryn Harrison
MR CROWL	Ian East
GEORGE	Alan Gill
MR CUTLER	Jeffery Dench
MRS CUTLER	Janet Dale
MRS KENWIGS' SISTER	Sharon Bower
LADY FROM DOWNSTAIRS	Rose Hill
MISS GREEN	Jane Downs
BENJAMIN	Teddy Kempner
PUGSTYLES	Roderick Horn
OLD LORD	Griffith Jones
YOUNG FIANCÉE	Juliet Hammond-Hill/Harriet Walter/Lucy Gutteridge
LANDLORD	Jeffery Dench

PORTSMOUTH

MR VINCENT CRUMMLES	Graham Crowden/Christopher Benjamin
MRS CRUMMLES	Lila Kaye
THE INFANT PHENOMENON	Julie Peasgood/Hilary Townley
MASTER PERCY CRUMMLES	Teddy Kempner
MASTER CRUMMLES	Mark Tandy
MRS GRUDDEN	Rose Hill
MISS SNEVELLICCI	Suzanne Bertish
MR FOLAIR	Timothy Spall/Clyde Pollitt
MR LENVILLE	Neil Phillips/Christopher Ravenscroft
MISS LEDROCK	Juliet Hammond-Hill/Harriet Walter/Lucy Gutteridge
MISS BRAVASSA	Sharon Bower
MR WAGSTAFF	Ben Kingsley/Fulton MacKay/Alun Armstrong
MR BLIGHTEY	Jeffery Dench
MISS BELVAWNEY	Janet Dale
MISS GAZINGI	Clare Travers-Deacon/Hilary Townley/Sally Nesbitt

MR PAILEY	William Maxwell
MR HETHERINGTON	Andrew Hawkins
MR BANE	Stephen Rashbrook
MR FLUGGERS	Griffith Jones
MRS LENVILLE	Shirley King
MR CURDLE	Hubert Rees
MRS CURDLE	Susan Littler/Emily Richard
MR SNEVELLICCI	John McEnery
MRS SNEVELLICCI	Thelma Whiteley

LONDON AGAIN

SCALEY	Clyde Pollitt/Ian McNeice
TIX	Teddy Kempner
SIR MULBERRY HAWK	Bob Peck
LORD FREDERICK VERISOPHT	Nicholas Gecks
MR PLUCK	Teddy Kempner
MR PYKE	John Matshikiza/Mark Tandy
MR SNOBB	Christopher Ravenscroft
COLONEL CHOWSER	Norman Tyrrell/Timothy Kightley
BROOKER	Clyde Pollitt
MR WITITTERLEY	Roderick Horn
MRS WITITTERLEY	Janet Dale
ALPHONSE	Stephen Rashbrook
OPERA SINGERS	Sharon Bower, Andrew Hawkins, John Woodvine
CHARLES CHEERYBLE	David Lloyd Meredith
NED CHEERYBLE	Hubert Rees
TIM LINKINWATER	Griffith Jones
THE MAN NEXT DOOR	Patrick Godfrey
KEEPER	Alan Gill
FRANK CHEERYBLE	Christopher Ravenscroft
NURSE	Thelma Whiteley
MADELINE BRAY	Juliet Hammond-Hill/Harriet Walter/Lucy Gutteridge
ARTHUR GRIDE	Jeffery Dench
WALTER BRAY	Norman Tyrrell/Christopher Benjamin
PEG SLIDERSKEW	Suzanne Bertish
HAWK'S RIVAL	Edward Petherbridge
CAPTAIN ADAMS	Andrew Hawkins
WESTWOOD	Neil Phillips/Alan Gill
CROUPIER	Timothy Spall/Ian McNeice
CASINO PROPRIETOR	Graham Crowden/Christopher Benjamin/Patrick Godfrey
SURGEON	Timothy Kightley
UMPIRE	Roderick Horn
POLICEMEN	Andrew Hawkins, Mark Tandy
MRS SNAWLEY	Janet Dale
YOUNG WOMAN	Clare Travers-Deacon/Hilary Townley

MUSICIANS MIKE STEER/ALAN GOUT *Music Director/Keyboards*, CHRISTOPHER LACEY *Flute*, VICTOR SLAYMARK *Clarinet*, PETER WHITTAKER *Bassoon*, PETER CAMERON *Trumpet*, RODERICK TEARLE *Trumpet*, DUNCAN HOLLOWOOD *Horn*, DAVID HISSEY *Trombone*, BRIDGET HIRST/WILFRID GIBSON *Violin*, ALASTAIR MCLACHLAN *Violin*, ALLEN WALLEY *Bass*, GEORGE WEIGAND *Guitar/Banjo*, TONY MCVEY *Percussion*, WEDDING ANTHEM SUNG BY CHORISTERS FROM ST. PAUL'S CATHEDRAL, *Master of the Choir* BARRY ROSE

UNDERSTUDY FOR THIRD RUN KATHARINE LEVY

ADAPTED BY DAVID EDGAR

DIRECTED BY TREVOR NUNN AND JOHN CAIRD

ASSISTED BY LEON RUBIN

DESIGNED BY JOHN NAPIER AND DERMOT HAYES

COSTUMES BY JOHN NAPIER

LIGHTING BY DAVID HERSEY

MUSIC AND LYRICS BY STEPHEN OLIVER

Stage Managers
PHILIP BASSETT/MICHAEL TOWNSEND
Deputy Stage Managers
DAVID PROCTOR/HILARY GROVES
Assistant Stage Manager
SIMON HOOPER

NICHOLAS NICKLEBY ran in London for three separate runs, from 6 June to 26 July 1980; 13 November 1980 to 3 January 1981; and 23 April to 20 June 1981.
As this book goes to press, this production is about to open on Broadway. Some slight cast changes may occur.

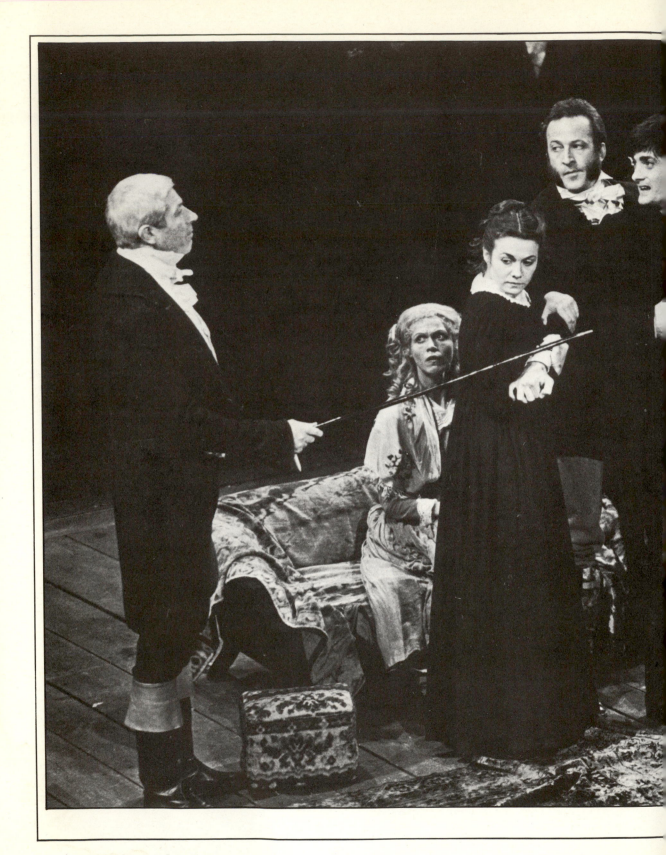